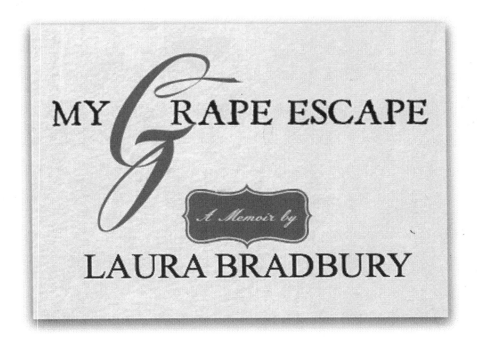

MY GRAPE ESCAPE

A Memoir by

LAURA BRADBURY

Bises!

Published by Grape Books

www.laurabradbury.com

ISBN 13: 978-0-9921583-0-9

À mon pirate et mes trois princesses, avec tout mon amour.

.

"Fais de ta vie un rêve, et d'un rêve, une réalité."

- de Antoine de Saint-Exupéry

PROLOGUE

Seconds after the little stone farmhouse - now officially ours - came into view my husband spoke. "Do you still refuse to believe in the Virgin Mary?"

I pressed my forehead against the rain-splattered window of the Citroën and took a closer look. The hollyhocks that had been in full bloom on the day of the sale were a distant memory and dark stains of humidity crept up the stucco. My hand found Franck's fingers. A section of the drainpipe had come loose - or maybe had been loose all along and we just hadn't noticed during the indigo days of summer. Water gushed down the corner of the house.

"So do you?" Frànck nodded towards the village's 12th century church across the street which housed a 16th century wood statue of this much revered lady. The Virgin of Magny-les-Villers was hardly as well known as the Virgin of Lourdes but it was rumoured among the villagers that she performed miracles all the same.

"I spent the last two years at Oxford being trained as a lawyer not a mystic," I replied. "Remember?"

"I remember." Franck's lips pressed together the way they did every time we discussed my law degree but his thumb caressed my palm. "Perhaps you would have been better off learning how to pray."

The car splashed through puddles the size of small lakes as we wound out of the village – *our* village now – of Magny-les-Villers and drove down the dip towards Villers-la-Faye. My plans didn't appear in quite the same idyllic light here in Burgundy as they did a continent and an ocean away in Vancouver.

"I can differentiate between a joint tenant and tenants in common and describe the mechanics of a discretionary trust."

"How exactly is that going to help us fix the stone steps?" He squeezed my hand. "*Non*. I need to teach you how to pray."

Pray? With the exception of that moment of insanity six months earlier that had propelled us down this uncharted road, I had been brought up to believe in strategy and hard work. I did not, like my husband and many of his fellow Burgundians, eschew logic in favour of miracles performed by ancient wooden statues.

"I don't need to become a Catholic," I said. "We just need to get organized and -"

"You saw the same thing I did out of the car window, didn't you?"

"You mean our house?"

"*Oui.*"

"Of course I did, but as I said, it will only take - "

"Divine intervention. That's the only way we're going to get that house ready by May."

I sank deeper in my seat. Granted, it was the dead of winter and we had exactly four months and ten days to prepare our house before the first group of holidaymakers arrived. We had a budget that covered around twenty per cent of the needed renovations with virtually no wiggle room for surprises. Franck had argued time and time again that, while houses like ours built in 1789 could never guarantee running water or even a single ninety degree angle, one thing they *did* guarantee was surprises. He hadn't been alluding to Roman coins hidden under the stairs but rather rotting walls and leaking septic tanks.

I pressed my forehead against the window again. The vines alongside the road were bare; only a scattering of workers hunched over them in vast rubber capes, miserable in the sheeting rain. We had a predicament. Worse yet, I knew it was entirely my fault.

"Talk to me about miracles," I said finally.

CHAPTER 1

Six months earlier I had hopped off the London train and landed on the platform in Beaune. We thought we'd be in Burgundy for a brief rest with Franck's family, a time for me to recover from the stress of my final law exams at Oxford.

Franck insisted I wait and let him deal with the luggage. The air smelled of wheat fields warmed by the sun and I felt my nerves untangle the tiniest bit. Franck shook his black hair from his eyes as he effortlessly heaved my eight suitcases down to the platform. I secretly marveled that I was actually married to this dashing Frenchman.

He waved at someone behind me and I turned to see his father André blanch as he caught sight of our fortification of luggage. Franck gave him a quick kiss on each cheek and then sped off in search of a much-needed cart or three. I considered justifying the number of suitcases but, though my French was excellent, I knew that when it came right down to it a reasonable explanation did not exist.

Franck and I had married in a miniscule Roman church in Burgundy the summer before; I was now officially André's daughter-in-law, but I knew I was still an unnerving presence for my quiet-spoken *beau-père*. There were too many things about me that smacked of my North American-ness: my need for long showers, lengthy phone conversations with my family back home, and, of course, travelling with ten times more stuff than a person actually required.

Despite any misgivings, André kissed me on each cheek and waited by my side, studiously avoiding any mention of my suitcases. Instead, he queried about the weather in Oxford and my recently passed exams.

Finally Franck reappeared, *sans* cart.

He clicked his tongue. "They've all been stolen."

I never had been able to comprehend the French compulsion to steal strange objects such as luggage carts and toilet seats just for the pure anarchist joy of thieving.

"We will just have to carry them ourselves," Franck said.

The final vestige of colour leeched from André's cheeks.

André watched in horror and I in awe as Franck, in an epic display of muscles and determination, attempted to shoehorn our luggage into André's compact Citroën.

Our intense and tenacious courtship should have tipped me off to my husband's inability to accept the word "impossible". We met on a blind date during the year I spent exploring the cafés of Beaune as a high school exchange student. He was four years older than I, a graduate of the Sorbonne, with flashing hazel eyes. I was the girl who had a surfeit of male friends but rarely an actual boyfriend. All at once a fairy tale romance became a defining part of my life.

This filled me with as much unease as it did wonder. I worried that any day fate would determine there had been a celestial mix-up. I hadn't *earned* Franck, particularly not during the past two years; I was the type of person who had to earn things.

"*Et voilà!*" Franck wedged the final suitcase in and stood back to admire his handiwork.

André ushered us into the car and we began to drive up towards the bright green vineyards of Franck's beloved *Hautes-Côtes*. I perched in the back on top of two suitcases, my head brushing the roof of the car. Franck rolled down the window to better breathe in his return home.

I had fallen madly in love with him from the moment he gave me the traditional *bises* on each cheek on the night we first met. I still loved him as much as I always had but I had spent my two years at Oxford buried under case books in the Bodleian Law Library while Franck zoomed back and forth to Paris on the Eurostar, taking society photos for the Moët et Chandon champagne company in Paris. We kept telling each other that we would have time to reconnect as soon as I walked out of my last final exam with the traditional red carnation in my buttonhole.

That moment had now come and gone.

Two days after we arrived, I was curled up in a ball on the bed in Franck's old bedroom, tucked away under the roof tiles and massive oak beams of chez Germain, his parents' stone house. Through the skylight above me a cloud shaped like an axe drifted by in an otherwise cornflower blue June sky.

We had been eating a delicious lunch of *poulet au madère* under the wisteria in the courtyard when my throat suddenly closed up. I had escaped from everyone at the lunch table so that I could be alone. I muttered something about stomach flu, staggered upstairs and collapsed on Franck's bed.

This wasn't my first panic attack - unfortunately. They had started a few weeks after I had begun my classes at Oxford. My grip on Franck's checked blue duvet tightened.

I had lain on this bed with Franck before, about two months after we first met. Our clothes had been more off than on when a whooshing noise above distracted me from our after lunch *sieste*. Franck was still preoccupied but I nudged him until he finally looked up. Then the pane of his skylight was obscured by scarlet fabric and we sat up, what little duvet we had over us falling away. The swath of red gave way to the faces of six hot-air balloon passengers out for a float over Burgundy's vineyards. They peered down at us through the skylight. Franck and I dived under the duvet and laughed until we couldn't breathe anymore.

That girl felt like someone I had not ever met before.

Now every muscle and tendon in my body reverberated from the effort of not giving in to the encroaching fear.

A cloud the shape of a staircase floated past. I had no choice but to keep going. I had to get into the Master's program at Oxford and then become a solicitor in London. Up. Up. Up. That had always been my life plan. My panic attacks couldn't be caused by anything exterior, I was certain. The strategy for my life remained perfectly sound - wealthy and successful London lawyers didn't have panic attacks. If I climbed the ladder of success high enough I would be safe, like in a childhood game of tag.

Franck's head ducked under the huge beam that framed the small passageway to his room. He came over and sat beside my curled form on the bed.

"*Attaque de panique?*" he asked and smoothed my hair away from my forehead.

I nodded, not wanting to burden him with my irrational terrors but at the same time feeling soothed by his presence.

"I thought they would go away when your exams were finished. " His fingers traced the lines of my jaw and circled around my left ear.

"So did I."

"Are you sure you don't want to come down? There is *Époisses* on the cheese platter. "

I lifted up my head slightly and rested it on his thigh. The waves of anxiety receded and my stubbornness surged in to take its place. I couldn't...I *wouldn't* let it win.

"What will I tell your family?"

"You don't need to tell them anything. In France it isn't unusual to leave the table because of a *malaise* and then come back. "

"Really?"

He shook his head, pulled me up and gave me a kiss. "Did I ever tell you the story of my mother's cousin Suzette who had to be carried off in a stretcher because of heart problems during an epic meal at her house?"

I laughed. "Seriously? Was she OK?"

"Not only was she OK, she made it back in time for the *choux à la crème* for dessert. "

CHAPTER 2

It was ten days later when, hand in hand, Franck and I walked through the frosty vineyards to meet our new nephew.

I couldn't believe that Franck's younger sister Stéphanie was actually a mother. She was only *my* age, twenty-five. Until then I had been the one to sally forth into new experiences: university in Montréal, volunteering in Nepal, law school at Oxford. But she had trumped me with this motherhood thing.

Stéphanie was one of the first people I met in France; she had orchestrated that initial blind date between Franck and I. She'd been telling me for months that I needed to meet her older brother, but I kept protesting that I was seeing someone else. This "someone else" was actually a guy I made out with furtively at every opportunity even though he didn't want us to be publicly known as boyfriend and girlfriend. Still, I had my pride, dammit. Only desperate people agreed to be set up on blind dates.

Stéphanie plunged ahead regardless of my protests and organized a *soirée* at a local *discothèque* with her brother, our mutual friend Sandrine, and one or two other friends from their village. I almost didn't show up at the appointed time on the main street of Nuits-Saint-Georges. The day before, I had come down with a sore throat and a runny nose. Seducing a total stranger was not high on my list of priorities.

Stéphanie leapt out of the car with her habitual verve, cigarette in hand. When she swung her shiny black hair out of her face and kissed me, I couldn't mistake the mischievous expression on her face.

Franck followed closely on her heels. His cheeky smile struck me first. He seemed to know that I would have preferred to stay at home (at that time I was living with a host family right beside the church in Nuits-Saint-Georges) but he was having none of such spiritless behaviour. He hadn't uttered a word, yet his eyes gleamed with a dare to join them.

I gave him the traditional *bises* on each cheek. He was cleanly shaven and his olive skin smelled vaguely of apples and wood chips. I hadn't expected Stéphanie's brother to be so handsome. *Devilishly* handsome. The cliché popped into my head out of nowhere, but I had to admit that with his lean muscles, chiselled facial bones and those flashing, almond shaped eyes it was accurate. My pride bolstered me up even as my heart sank. Men like Franck were invariably bad news.

I stepped back and cocked an appraising eyebrow. "I've heard a lot about you," I said.

Franck's brows flew up for a split, but gratifying, second. He laughed. "*Bon.* I guess I have a lot to live up to."

"I guess you do."

Franck took my hand and pulled me down into the backseat of the car beside him.

We had all changed in the past eight years. Stéphanie had dropped her prodigious smoking habit and her wild ways and was now the mother of a little boy named Tom. As for that daring girl I had been, I missed her.

Tom's birth had been rough - a protracted labour followed by an emergency C-section. Stéphanie and Tom had just been released from the hospital that very morning. I still found it odd to be descending on new parents for a drink, but Franck insisted that it was an absolute obligation to "*arroser la naissance du petit*" with a *kir*.

"Stéph must be exhausted," I said as we passed a tiny chapel housing only a statue of the Virgin Mary strategically positioned in the vineyards mid-way between the two villages of Magny-les-Villers and Villers-la-Faye. "Surely they just want some privacy?"

Franck cast me an odd look that made me realize, even before he spoke, that my view was the polar opposite of how a Burgundian would think.

"It's good luck to drink to the baby's health. They would be disappointed if nobody showed up." Franck's index finger twitched on his right hand – his smoking hand. He'd given up his daily package of cigarettes ten months ago but I could always tell from that finger twitch when a craving struck. "When we have kids we'll probably be in England, so you won't have to worry that everyone will reciprocate."

He didn't quite manage to hide the longing in his voice. Children. Franck was ready for them and had been for at least two years. I wanted them too - eventually - but I still had so much climbing to do before we embarked on that journey.

We walked up the gravel path to Stéphanie and Thierry's house. The steeple of Magny-les-Villers' church was painted silver with frost. Its bell reverberated four times as it rang the hour. The more delicate bell of the village hall echoed it a minute later.

Stéphanie opened their front door. Her green eyes sported dark circles and her hair hung limp down her back, but a deep sense of contentment glowed underneath the fatigue. A wave of jealousy washed over me. I longed for the bliss she was feeling – the bliss I *thought* I had earned by finishing my final exams.

I kissed both her and Thierry, stuttered out my *felicitations*, then quickly took a spot on a floor cushion in front of the roaring fireplace.

Thierry, his face red with a mixture of pride and the drinks with the numerous visitors who had apparently beaten us to the punch, poured us all a celebratory *kir*. Stéphanie brought Tom over and settled in on the couch near us by the fire to nurse him, promising we could hold and admire him after he had been fed. Thierry hopped up to stoke the fire so neither of them would be cold and Stéphanie laughed at his fussing. My own life, steeped in the stress of grades and academia, seemed so sterile in comparison.

I looked up to see Stéphanie thrusting Tom into my arms. She didn't notice how badly my hands were shaking. I clutched my nephew against my chest, certain that I was going to drop him otherwise. He lay there like a limpet, undisturbed by the confusion roaring underneath my breastbone. His clearly etched half-moon brows were the same colour as his thatch of black hair.

"It suits you to have a baby in your arms!" Stéphanie said. "When are you going to give him a cousin?" She planted a kiss on Thierry's mouth. Tom began to squirm and chirp like a discontented bird.

Stéphanie leaned over me and plucked him out of my arms. "Are you hungry again *petit monstre*?" I didn't realize how much I enjoyed his warmth and weight against me until it was gone. Without Tom to distract me, the panic began to crush me beneath its heel again. Now that all the hard work of my law degree was completed, where was my contentment?

The next morning I didn't wake up with the sudden courage to veer off the planned course of my life. By the time I went to sleep that night, however, I was — much to my surprise - forty thousand dollars richer.

It all began with a phone call to my parents. I wasn't even calling about money. I was calling because I thought I was going crazy.

My anxiety was something I had never accepted in myself. It was not a face I wanted to show to anybody, especially not my parents, but the panic attacks had been as relentless as pounding waves over the past few days, eroding everything solid except the precipice of sanity I teetered upon. It was with a mix of desperation and dread that I picked up the receiver.

My father answered. After a few minutes of beating around the bush, I broke down and it all came out in a torrential rush: how I was sure I was going insane, how I was certain it must be deathly serious if I felt this bad, how I knew something was terribly wrong.

As I confessed my misery, cords of guilt tightened around me. My parents had supported me, not only financially but emotionally, through my two years at Oxford. I had no right to be such a mess.

Dizziness forced me to pause for breath.

"Laura," my father said, "I have felt like you are feeling right now."

I had already written and directed a scenario in my head where my father demanded to speak to Franck and then convinced him to haul me off to the nearest psychiatric facility; I had not expected this.

"You have?"

"Yes. In fact, I'm probably the one who is responsible for the tendency towards anxiety in your DNA." I grabbed this like a life preserver. "Sorry about that," he added.

"I feel like I'm going to die or something awful is going to happen.
"

"You've just been chronically stressed for a long time."

"What should I do?"

"Go to the doctor," he said. "Tell him exactly what you just told me. Ask for some Valium and take them as prescribed. Try to relax and find a new project. Trust me, you *will* feel better. "

My relief was so overpowering that I had to sit down on the floor. All of a sudden reality snapped back into place. Everything lost its distorted, menacing edge. It was like finding the exit from the fun house after having been trapped inside for far too long.

"You promise to go to the doctor tomorrow?" he pressed.

"I promise," I said, even though I could already understand the temptation not to follow through. Everything seemed fine now.

"Promise to call me when you get back from seeing him?"

"I promise."

"Oh, I almost forgot," he said. "Your grandfather just gave forty thousand dollars to your sister to help them finish off their renovations. He wants to give you the same amount so things are fair. His cheque is here at the office waiting for you. Do you want me to invest it somewhere safe until you decide what you want to do with the money?"

"Forty thousand dollars?" I had never received such a windfall before.

"That's right."

"No strings attached?" That did not sound like my grandfather.

"That's what he said," my father answered. "But knowing your grandfather, he'll let you know loud and clear if you put it somewhere he doesn't like. Do you want my advice?"

"Sure."

"Real estate. He'll love it and it's always a good investment."

"An apartment in Oxford?" I wondered out loud, but even as I said it every cell in my body rebelled against the idea.

"I don't think you'd be able to buy a dog shed for that price in Oxford, or here in Victoria for that matter. Anyway, there's no rush. Take care of yourself first. The money isn't going anywhere."

I got off the phone feeling, maybe not one hundred per cent, but definitely one hundred per cent *better* than when I had picked up the receiver to call him.

"Forty thousand," Franck murmured as we lay in bed that night, my head nestled in the curve of his shoulder. "That's not the kind of thing that happens every day."

It was a complete windfall. Part of me was deliriously happy, but another part felt uneasy. Such good luck made me conspicuous. It made me stick out just a little bit farther in destiny's Rolodex. I wondered if fate would notice me now, scrutinize my card, and think, "Laura needs something nasty to happen to her to even things out."

Behind that thought, though, an idea began to percolate.

The next morning I was sure I would completely recover on my own - I wished I hadn't promised my father that I would go to the doctor. Franck had gone ahead and made the appointment with their family doctor before I had even emerged from bed.

Thanks to my overactive imagination, doctor's visits had always filled me with terror. By the time Franck checked his watch and informed me it was time to go I was fighting the urge to bring up my breakfast. In another frame of mind, the drive would have been stunning. The sun was shining, but to me the vineyards we passed seemed to get darker the further we drove. Franck rolled his window down and enjoyed the fresh breeze until we passed the sign which welcomed us to the little village of Ladoix-Serrigny. He parked beside what looked like a stone house on the main village square. On one side of the house I noticed a set of crumbling stone stairs that led nowhere, something I would normally have found charming but which now struck me as ominous.

"What kind of doctor is he?" I hissed at Franck as we crunched on the gravel path leading to the door. I was fighting the image of a man closely resembling Gerard Depardieu at his most dissolute coming at me with a tranquilizer dart and a straightjacket.

"Le Père Dupont?" Franck asked, surprised. Like the rest of his family, Franck often called his doctor "Father Dupont", as if he was a priest or something. This didn't help me - I'd always found priests almost as unnerving as doctors. "He's just about the least intimidating person on earth."

I could never understand why other people didn't find doctors terrifying. Who else could have the power to announce to you that you would be dead in a month's time from an untreatable condition? To make matters worse, this doctor was French. He would probably make me take all my clothes off in order to take my blood pressure or something.

I was a sweating, mute disaster by the time the Docteur Dupont came out in the waiting room and called my name.

He and Franck chatted for a few interminable minutes about England while I endevoured not to pass out. I got the vague impression Docteur Dupont did look a tad like Gerard Depardieu, less about forty pounds, but I couldn't see clearly beyond the spots swimming in front of my eyes.

"What brings you here today, Madame Germain?" the doctor finally asked after Franck and I had been ushered into his office.

I opened my mouth, but no words came out.

"Laura needs some valium," Franck said, then reached over and squeezed my hand.

Oh My God. That was as good as admitting that I *was* crazy.

"*Ah bon?*" The doctor cocked his head, nonplussed, as if people came in to ask for Valium every day. Then it struck me like a thunderbolt. Maybe people *did* come to ask for valium every day.

I tried to explain myself in the awkward pigeon French that always came out of my mouth at the precise moments when I most needed polish. "You see, I just finished my law degree in England. It was very stressful. I'm still waiting for the results for my final exams… I'm not usually like this you know…I don't know what's wrong with me. I feel terrible all the time, like something dreadful is going to happen and - "

"You need a good *relaxant*," the doctor interrupted. He motioned me over behind a screen where there was an examination table and a blood pressure cuff hooked on the wall. "First come over here, if it pleases you."

I walked unsteadily behind him. It didn't please me at *all* as a matter of fact. Just looking at the cuff made me want to pass out. I knew that every time I was within five hundred feet of a doctor's office my blood pressure went through the roof.

He put the cuff on and began to pump it up. I shut my eyes and tried to conjure up the ubiquitous tropical beach with swaying palm trees but I couldn't concentrate on anything but my heart beating far too fast. If only I could *control* my thoughts. My face was bright red from the effort of trying but I was failing miserably. I couldn't bear to look at the doctor's face when the cuff deflated. The Velcro crackled through the silence as he took it off.

"A bit on the high side, but then I'd wager that happens to you often at the doctor's office, *n'est-ce pas*? The medicine I am going to prescribe you should help. Life can be very much nicer with *relaxants*."

That switch flicked inside me like the day before - the anxiety was gone. It had simply vanished. All that was left was me, sitting on an examination table, feeling like a fool.

I hung my head and noticed for the first time that under his impressive girth Docteur Dupont was schlepping around in a pair of tatty espadrilles. How could I have been so terrified of someone wearing *espadrilles*?

He ushered me back to his desk where Franck sat, watching me.

"Is she going to live?" he asked, adopting a morose tone belied by the sparkle in his eyes.

Le Père Dupont chuckled. "I don't see why not." He scribbled something on his prescription pad. "Better yet, if Madame Germain takes one of these three times a day until she is feeling better she may actually begin to enjoy life too."

He pushed the prescription over to me. His chunky fingers reached out and patted mine. "It happens to all of us from time to time, you know. It's what makes us human. We are not meant to be *des machines*."

Just then, the roar of a vineyard tractor filled the doctor's office.

"Can she drink wine with the pills?" Franck asked.

I turned to Franck, horrified. Any doctor I knew in either Canada or England would deem his question ridiculous at best, irresponsible at worst. Health came first, of course. Enjoyment of things like *wine* shouldn't even be a consideration.

"Only *good* wine," Docteur Dupont answered. "I would highly recommend around two glasses at lunch and dinner. Something fortifying. A *Pommard* or a *Vosne-Romanée* would be perfect, though I would also consider a solid *Savigny*. I would, however, advise you to stay away from the whites at the moment, Madame Germain. They tend to have an agitating effect. "

Franck nodded and gave me a wink.

"You know what they say here in Burgundy?" The Doctor's brown eyes met mine and twinkled.

"*Quoi?*"

"Nothing makes the future look so rosy as to contemplate it through a glass of *Chambertin*." He stood up and ushered us out. The village church bell was chiming eleven o'clock. "I think that was our wise little Napoleon who said that. If only the state would reimburse it, I would write several prescriptions for *Chambertin* a day."

When I got home I felt, for the first time in months, back to my old self. So much so that I didn't want to take my little pill, but Franck threatened that if I didn't follow the prescription he would phone Le Père Dupont *and* my father to rat me out.

Franck's parents didn't have any *Chambertin* on hand, so I took my evening pill along with a glass of lovely Savigny-les-Beaune *Les Guettes* made by one of Franck's many uncles. I lay dozing in a lawn chair after dinner. The setting sun lit up the wisteria from above; summer air caressed my skin. Yesterday the world had seemed like a small, black room but now, with some help from the wine and Docteur Dupont's pills, it became a place of endless possibility.

CHAPTER 3

I had never thought enjoying a cherry *tarte* outside under the wisteria would be such a challenge. It was all the fault of the cherry pits. Mémé, Franck's grandmother, was the one who had baked the *tarte* and it was her steadfast belief that cherry pits should be left in the fruit.

"It is the only way to get the best flavour!" she explained to me in loud tones that carried into the living room where Michèle, Franck's mother, had retreated.

"There's nothing that annoys me more than picking the pits out of a cherry *tarte*," Michèle riposted. "Besides, they add nothing whatsoever to the flavour."

When our *lapin à la moutarde* and a half round of *Cîteaux* were sufficiently honoured, Mémé strode back into the kitchen to get her *tarte*. She presented it with great flourish and cut everyone a large slice. It looked delicious and I was determined, now that I was feeling better, to savour every pleasure I encountered on my daily path.

Mémé began to chew hers with sounds of ecstasy that were unmistakably aimed at her daughter. Michèle, meanwhile, picked each pit out of her mouth with a grimace and lined them up disdainfully, like a row of suspects, on the napkin beside her plate.

The silence between mother and daughter made the dappled sunlight of the table under the wisteria feel like the Gaza strip. Franck plowed through his piece unperturbed. Franck's father André, meanwhile, polished off his slice in record time and excused himself to go into the house to do the dishes. My gaze shifted nervously from

17

Mémé to Michèle. I took another wary bite and tried to chew as though I was enjoying it…but not too much.

After lunch I climbed up to Franck's room and flopped on the duvet. Through his skylight clouds gamboled past in a blue sky, blissfully unaware of the cherry pit storm still brewing below. I picked up the bottle of pills Le Père Dupont had prescribed me that were sitting on the miniature wine barrel serving as a bedside table. The prescription said to take one or two more a day in times of anxiety. Did this count? I put the bottle back down. The stressful things that happened outside of me were nothing compared to the stressful feelings inside my own head. I would save the pills for those.

My thoughts drifted to my husband, who was undoubtedly now working his way through a second or maybe even third piece of cherry *tarte*, his digestion unperturbed by the tension around the table. A few minutes later Franck bent down and made his way through the tiny opening to his garret of a bedroom. He came down and sat beside where I was still lying.

"Is the anxiety back?" he brushed the hair off my forehead.

"*Non*," I said and pulled him down beside me so I could nestle my head in the crook of his shoulder. "I was just thinking about your mother and your grandmother down there. Did you even notice they were fighting?"

"*That* wasn't fighting."

"What constitutes fighting around here?"

Franck considered this for a moment. "When things start to get thrown around."

"Doesn't conflict make you feel uncomfortable?"

Franck stared at me in amazement. "*Bien sûr que, non*. If everyone got along all the time life would be unbearably boring. Besides, there are six of us in the house right now – what did you expect?"

"Wouldn't it be great to have our own little place here?" I mused. "We could come and visit and enjoy everyone without living in each other's pockets."

I remembered the forty thousand dollars from my grandfather. We would always want to return to Burgundy to visit with Franck's family and our friends. Burgundy was in Franck's blood and it had filtered into mine as well. Sometimes we would want to come for long periods of time…

I touched the stone wall of Franck's room and thought about how long ago those stones has been stacked. Centuries ago. I loved the old buildings in France. Most of them had been built before the Europeans even reached the coast in my part of the world. A flame of something forgotten ignited in me.

"Maybe we should start looking for a little place of our own here." I lifted my head to get a better view of my husband's reaction.

Franck gave a start but after considering this idea for a while he leaned over and kissed me back against the duvet.

"I found something!" Franck came rushing in through the front gate just before dinner the next day, followed by his father whom he had picked up on his way home from Beaune.

His triumph rendered him oblivious to the deep freeze that had settled like hoarfrost around the kitchen table. As far as I could tell, the Cherry Pit Incident had never been fully resolved; just five minutes ago Mémé had criticized how Michèle always let Franck's little brother Emmanuel-Marie have ketchup on his pasta.

Emmanuel-Marie, with all the perfidy of a nine-year-old, got up to go to the bathroom and took the ketchup bottle with him. Franck's mother had conceived him twenty years after Franck, following a brutal treatment for a rare and deadly form of cancer that struck her at thirty-five. According to the doctors, her disease should have killed her, not to mention rendered her sterile several times over. During her illness and treatment Michèle had travelled to Lourdes and prayed to the Virgin Mary for help. The pugnacious towhead emerging from the bathroom, pulling up his shorts with one hand and clutching his bottle of Heinz with the other, was tangible proof that those prayers to the Virgin Mary were answered.

Franck flipped open the pad of paper he had been carrying. I glanced over but couldn't decipher any of his scrawls.

"On my way down to Beaune I drove around a little," he began. "I saw a sign in Marey-les-Fussey in front of a house for sale. Maybe two houses actually, on an incredible piece of land looking on to the vineyards."

My heart started to beat a little faster - from excitement rather than panic for a change.

"I've got the number for the real estate agent. From the sign it looked like he was from Châlon. It was the *only* house I saw for sale, and the fact that it is in Marey-les-Fussey..." Franck caught my eye. "I believe it's a sign."

No-one at the table rolled their eyes at the talk of signs. Mémé and Michèle both nodded and waited to hear more. Signs and divine intervention were par for the course for Franck's family; Emmanuel-Marie was sitting right beside us, after all.

I hadn't been brought up to pray to the Virgin Mary, or anyone else, but now I realized that Franck had most likely been praying to her since last night for the right house to fall across our path. He always carried a well-worn icon of the Virgin Mary in his leather wallet. He lived his life convinced that he was not only protected by the Virgin but also by an assorted crew of deceased grandparents, uncles, and a friend or two up in Heaven. He considered this motley celestial crew to be his guardian angels.

Like so many North Americans, my upbringing had been heavy on the morality and light on the spirituality, whereas for Franck, like many French people, it had been the opposite.

"Marey?" Mémé frowned and tapped her fingers on the tabletop. "It is filled with *Poiriers*. They've always been *compliqués* as far as families go."

Michèle pursed her lips in agreement. It was true that at least half the village was populated by one extended family but this didn't worry me – I was just relieved that uniting against the villagers of Marey had apparently smoothed over the question of Emmanuel-Marie's love for ketchup.

"Where is it in relation to the church?" Michèle asked.

She meant the church where Franck and I had been married a year before. It was a little stone affair dating back to Roman times with a rounded ceiling and scarred wooden benches located near the end of the village, or the beginning, depending on which direction you were coming from. The floor was made up of flagstones so worn with time that they were polished smooth with the details of the knights that had been buried beneath them several centuries ago carved in Old French.

A house for sale in Marey when Marey only consisted of about twenty houses . . while I couldn't bring myself to believe that the Virgin Mary or any guardian angels were looking out for *me*, I could believe they had thrown Franck this gift.

Franck grabbed the ketchup bottle and poured some over his pasta, then dug in while Michèle and Mémé both pretended not to notice.

The next morning, after polishing off our *café au lait* and *tartines* of jam made from the wild peaches that grew in the vineyards, Franck began pacing around the kitchen.

"Do you think it's too early to call?"

I checked my watch. "It's only ten after seven."

Franck grimaced. "How early do you think is too early?"

"Before eight thirty is definitely too early."

"What am I going to do before then?" Franck raised his arms towards the ceiling and I supposed beyond that to those guardian angels of his.

"Have a shower. Have another *café au lait*. Give me a shoulder massage." He stopped to laugh at my saucy smile but then resumed his pacing. I began to heat up some more milk in the saucepan, stirring it slowly with a worn wooden spoon.

"How can you stand to wait?" he demanded after a few minutes.

I was eager too, of course, but there was some sort of inner calm that had descended over me since the night before. I had no idea where it had come from.

"I don't know," I said. "I guess I just feel that if this house is meant to be, it'll work out no matter what time we call the realtor."

Franck drew to an abrupt halt. "How many of those pills have you had this morning?"

"None." In fact, I had woken up with my thoughts so consumed by beautiful old doors and views over the vineyards that I had completely forgotten to take them. "I don't know why I feel so calm about all of this," I admitted. "I want it just as much as you do."

Franck peered at me. "Do you feel like it will work out for the best one way or the other?" he ventured.

I almost felt scared as I let the word out of my mouth, as if I was going to jinx myself.

"*Oui*," I admitted.

"You know what's that called?"

"Insanity?"

He clicked his tongue. "*Ma chérie*, it's called faith."

I stood beside Franck as he talked on the phone, wishing that his parents hadn't updated their phone system around the time of our wedding and done away with their old orange phone with the separate earpiece called an *écouteur* so I could eavesdrop on the conversation. All I could do was watch Franck's face as he listened to the realtor. It lit up within a few seconds and stayed lit.

After he hung up, he grabbed my hands and led me in an impromptu little two-step until he whacked his head on the beam that ran across the low ceiling of the *cellier*. "*Merde!*" he rubbed his forehead but nothing could wipe off his smile.

"What did the realtor say? What's it like?" I pressed.

"It sounds *incroyable*! The property is huge and goes all the way down to the vineyards and there are actually *two* separate houses on it."

"How much are they asking?" I asked.

"Three hundred and twenty thousand *francs*."

He watched my expression while I engaged in a series of quick mental calculations. Three hundred and twenty thousand francs - that was about $100,000 Canadian. From Franck's description of the property, it sounded like a downright steal. Of course, that didn't change the fact that it was still a fortune for Franck and me; we had no real source of income between the two of us. We had forty thousand for a down payment though, which would make the mortgage quite small...

I should have been terrified about our ability to pay the monthly mortgage payments, but somehow I just wasn't. Compared to the dark phantoms flitting in and out of my mind over the past two years, dealing with concrete dollars and cents, or *francs* in this case, was a relief.

Besides, my conviction that we could make this work one way or another was still there. I wasn't ready to call it faith yet, and I had no idea why my confidence manifested itself in French real estate rather than in God, but there it was.

CHAPTER 4

We visited the property in Marey-les-Fussey the next morning. The realtor was driving in from Châlon-sur-Saone, about half an hour south and the only free slot he could give us was eleven o'clock. Right away would have suited us much better, but we reminded ourselves that it wouldn't do to appear desperate.

We walked to Marey-les-Fussey, only a leisurely ten minute stroll through the vineyards from Villers-la-Faye; we arrived a half hour early. We had driven by the sprawling property about a dozen times the day before so we knew exactly where we were headed.

I crossed the street to walk right up to the front gate of the property. It looked deserted. The agent had told Franck that the sellers, two elderly sisters, had already moved into a nursing home. The red tiled roofs and the old stone well in the courtyard seemed to be calling me. Franck grabbed my arm and yanked me back into the shadows on the other side of the street.

"Everyone in the village will be watching," he hissed. I surveyed the empty cobblestone thoroughfare. A vineyard tractor rumbled in the distance but that was the only sign of human life. "In here!" Franck ducked under the thick stone walls of the village washing house and pulled me in behind him.

"What's wrong with just walking around the yard of the house?" I asked, blinking as my eyes adjusted to the dark. "Nobody's there." It wasn't like Franck, or any other French person for that matter, to be so rule-abiding.

"We mustn't be seen," he answered in a whisper. "Or overheard."

There was a little round window looking out to the street. I stood on my tiptoes and peered out. Still no sign of life except a few chickens clucking around a grassy patch two houses down.

"There's nobody out there, unless you're worried the chickens are spying on us."

"Trust me. They're there even if you can't see them."

"Who?"

"The villagers. They'll be watching us. That's how it is in *ces villages*."

Franck was always full of tales of the mysterious workings of *ces villages*, or "these villages", but I remained sceptical. I looked out of the window again. It was just past ten thirty but the day was already so hot that waves of heat shimmered over the cobblestones and seemed to slide down the slopes of the vineyards that dropped from the village on either side of the road. There were worse places to wait than under the cool of the ancient *lavoir*, to be sure, but I still couldn't believe there was any need for cloak and dagger furtiveness.

"Even if the villagers *are* watching us," I countered, though I was far from convinced, "surely we're allowed to visit a house that's for sale, aren't we? Or is there a law against that that I wasn't aware of?"

He reached over and pulled me against his firm chest. "It's not that." He nipped my earlobe. "The fact is that if they see us visiting the property they will start to think they should take more interest in it. They'll steal it from under our noses."

"Why would they want another huge property when they all own a house in the village already?"

"To keep an outsider from buying in their village."

"You're not an outsider. You're from one village over."

Franck's eyes flashed in the dim light. "I might as well be from outer Siberia. Don't forget the fact that I also married an *etrangère*."

The roar of a car engine drowned out the chickens' clucks. Franck used one strong arm to pin me against the wall while he peeked out. Cool humidity seeped through my T-shirt and a pointed rock poked into my back.

"It's him," Franck released me. We emerged from our hiding spot and tried to walk as nonchalantly as we could across the blistering road.

As we approached the black car that had pulled up in front of the gate, a red-faced man stumbled out of the driver's seat. A file folder full of papers slid out and scattered over the dusty ground. Franck collected them swiftly, passed them back to the realtor, and stuck out his hand.

"*Bonjour.*"

The real estate agent was still muttering vague *mercis* and *merdes* and *fais-chiers* but managed to get a solid enough grip on his file to shake Franck's hand.

"*Vous êtes Franck Germain?*"

"*Oui.* This is *ma femme*, Laura."

Being introduced as Franck's wife was only a year old and still gave me a shiver of pleasure. There was a caveman possessiveness about the word "wife" in French; the word *femme* meant both "my wife" and "my woman" at the same time.

The agent clasped my hand in his moist paw and then began to forage deep in his pocket for the key to the front gate. Franck was quivering with the need to get us out of the villagers' sight. We all sighed in relief when after a seemingly interminable time the realtor extracted the key and used it to unlock the front gate.

"So you're from Châlon," Franck said, his voice low as we walked into the grassy yard between the two houses. "This is a bit far away for you. Do you represent a lot of sellers in this area?"

The agent shook his head. "Almost never. Completely out of my *secteur*, this is, but it is being sold by some old ladies who are friends of my mother. I'm doing it as a favour but to tell you the truth it's a bit of a pain."

He led us, or rather was hustled onwards by Franck, into the first house that ran low-slung across the back of the yard.

He unlocked the door using a huge iron key and I stepped on to flagstones that had been perfectly polished with time and wear. The room was beautifully cool. From what I knew of these old Burgundian houses, the walls were undoubtedly made with stones equally as thick and massive. The kitchen was sparse and simple but I loved everything about it: the scratched wooden cabinets, the huge double ceramic sink, even the spiral fly tape that was dotted with several large, expired victims. The back of my neck prickled; I swear I could almost feel the sweet breath of Franck's guardian angels.

We continued on to the other rooms. The house was small but oozing with potential. There was the fabulous kitchen, *bien sûr*, and then a bedroom with a deep patina in the wooden floors. I could completely look past the mustard and green velvet wallpaper, the cross complete with an impaled Jesus over the headboard, and the dried and very dusty bridal bouquet under an even dustier glass dome on the bedside table. Next to the bedroom was a small water closet with a sink but no other bathroom; I wondered where the previous occupants had washed – in the well? Next was a separate living area set off by a massive stone fireplace.

Franck didn't say a word but from the determined set of his mouth I knew he wasn't missing a thing.

The first house was slung perpendicular to the main road through the village, whereas, the second house was completely vertical. It was much newer too, according to the realtor, meaning it had been built a mere two centuries ago instead of four.

The second house had four floors. Each floor had one or two rooms, and they were connected by a graceful wooden staircase that spiralled up the middle of the structure and became steeper the higher we climbed. The final room – a bedroom under the eaves of the roof - took up the entire top floor. A perfect spot, I thought, to come and escape from the world with a book on a rainy day…once the dead flies were cleaned up. The carpet and the windowsill were dotted with them.

Once the house tours were done, the realtor showed us through the first of two massive stone outbuildings which had been used as barns for a few hundred years. Inside, we discovered a rusting motor scooter, an old wooden cart that was missing two wheels, and four giant glass bottles used for distilling *poire william* and other hard alcohols.

"These *granges* can also be renovated and made into other houses," the realtor said, caressing the wall. It was true, the stone and massive oak beams provided an amazing canvas for another house altogether.

The farthest outbuilding commanded a view of the entire valley where yellow wheat fields gave way to vineyards and then back to fields again, topped off by a ridge of green trees. Inside, a rickety wooden ladder was propped up against a wooden overhang. Franck squinted up its length, swung his leg over, and began to shimmy up.

The realtor called up to him, "Can't guarantee that it is safe up there, you know! You could come through the floorboards - probably completely rotten." Franck had already disappeared from the top of the ladder.

"Laura, come up here!" he called down to me.

"I wouldn't if I were you," the realtor advised.

"What if I fall through the floorboards?" I called up to Franck.

"I'll catch you."

While the realtor shook his head I put my foot on the first rung and began to gingerly make my way up. How much scarier could this really be than climbing the stairs of Oxford's Examination Schools before my first final exam? Whatever waited for me up top, it couldn't be as bad as the vertiginous feeling of terror and uncertainty I had felt then.

Hope flickered inside me - this splintering old ladder might lead me to a completely different kind of place. Besides, this was perhaps the only chance for Franck and me to whisper our opinions to each other away from the realtor.

I pushed thoughts of rotting floorboards and termites from my mind and scrabbled up the last few rungs. Such worries were slightly unnerving, but in a reassuring, concrete way. They were infinitely preferable to the other kind of doubts that had been running in a continuous loop through my mind in the past two years.

My head poked out just over the level of the wooden beams and Franck, a grin on his face, grabbed my hand and pulled me up beside him. He led me, boards creaking ominously under our feet, to the far end of the mezzanine and a little waist high stone wall. His arm wrapped around my shoulders as we gazed out at an uninterrupted view over the vineyards. He kissed my earlobe.

"You could write here."

I fingered an ivy leaf from the vine that perfectly framed the view.

"I can't believe how perfect it is," I whispered back. I could become someone else here. Still…how could we possibly make it work? How was I supposed to live here and also finish my Masters at Oxford and establish a legal career in London?

But this place was perfect. Everything about buying the property seemed so easy and self-evident, as though it was meant to be. Even if I was miserable practising law, it would enable us to keep this unbelievable place. How could anything go truly bad when I owned as magical a place as this? Desperation to make this dwelling my own made my bones ache.

Franck must have sensed the sudden urgency in my mood because he gave my earlobe one last nip and tilted his head towards the real estate agent pacing below us.

"Don't let on how much we like it," he murmured. "He'll realize that he's priced it too low." I nodded.

We made our way back down the ladder and Franck lost no time in telling the realtor that indeed most of the floorboards *had* been rotten up there. "Termites, *sans doute*," he concluded offhandedly.

I followed as Franck led us all back to the first low-slung house and pointed at the roofline. "That house will need to be entirely re-roofed."

Now that Franck pointed it out, I noticed that the tiles did undulate like a wave.

Franck clicked his tongue. "The beams will probably have to be replaced as well."

We made our way back towards the gate as Franck enumerated the herculean amount of repairs required, the epic number of hours it would take every week to mow the very substantial chunk of land, and the constant danger of children falling down the very charming old stone well that Franck laid his hand on as he came to a stop.

I hadn't noticed any of these things before, but I couldn't deny that they were all true. My palm itched to slap Franck. He was ruining the spell the property had cast over me, even if it was merely to put the realtor off our scent. This house was destined for us, despite the roof and the rot and the backbreaking lawn mowing.

As Franck gave the well a final, dismissive pat I felt a piercing pain under my baby toe. The pain hop scotched down the sole of my foot. I dropped to the grass and clawed off my left sandal. A half-squished wasp fell out onto the grass.

I gave an explosive demonstration of my command of French swear words. It had been years since I'd been stung and I'd forgotten how much it hurt. Not just the pain, but the burning and the itching that made me want to tear off my foot.

"*C'est quoi?*" Franck leaned over me.

"*Une guêpe,*" I swore one last time and then took Franck's proffered arm and hobbled back to our car. I noticed twitching curtains at the three houses across the street. Maybe Franck hadn't been completely wrong about the spying villagers after all.

By the time I collapsed in the scorching leather car seat my foot was beginning to swell. What could this mean? Franck's guardian angels were sending distinctly mixed signals. The perfect house, a feeling of nearly captured peace, then a wasp sting. That was the problem with believing in signs; if I believed in the good signs from the heavens, I felt honor-bound to believe the bad signs too. Only Franck could have such mercurial guardian angels.

Mémé made me press a vinegar compress against my foot for a good hour after getting back to chez Franck. The pain subsided gradually, leaving the more painful contemplation of what such an omen meant - and it would take more imagination than I possessed to believe it a good one.

CHAPTER 5

The wasp sting had not only made my foot swell up and itch like the *diable*, but it had split my brain in two. On one hand, I was desperate to cling to the belief that any problems with the Marey property would magically work themselves out with the assistance of Franck's guardian angels and the Virgin Mary. Each throb of my foot, however, reminded me of all the things Franck had pointed out to the realtor – the warped roof, the grotty wallpaper, not to mention the need to rewire the entire house. The money we had to put as a deposit on the house was finite. Neither Franck nor I had a job or really any prospects of one.

Franck, on the other hand, had no problem believing in only the good omens and discarding the bad. He had already moved us to Marey in his mind.

"We could do a B&B, or a *chambres-d'hôtes*!" he said, handing me a freshly soaked vinegar cloth. "I'll set up that little room for you in the *grange* and you can write fabulous articles and *pourquoi pas* a novel?"

I longed to be swept away with Franck and his plans but my burning foot tethered me to the ground.

"What if the property is so cheap because it's defective?"

The idea had obviously not occurred to him. "Defective? How could that be?"

"I don't know. I've never bought a house before. Terrible neighbours could be another possibility."

"The neighbour is Victor's brother. I grew up with him. He and his wife are *charmants*. They make honey for a living."

I thought for a few seconds more. "What if there are Roman ruins under the ground?"

Franck went pale at this, as I suspected he would. When Franck was just a small boy his grandfather had found some Roman coins while tilling his vineyards. He gave them to Franck on the condition that Franck was sworn to secrecy. Finding Roman artefacts or ruins was a real problem in Burgundy. If word got out, the government and the archaeologists would get involved and the upshot would be the expropriation of land - a thing to be avoided at all costs.

"I know my dad always has properties inspected before offering to purchase anything," I said to Franck who was still drawing his brows together over the Roman ruins scenario. "Do you think we could do that?"

"Maybe," Franck conceded. "But I have no idea how to go about it." His family didn't know any more than we did. Franck's parents had inherited their house from Michèle's father, who had inherited it from his mother, who had inherited it from her family and so on and so forth back through the centuries. Like many villagers, they had never bought or sold a house in their lives.

We spent the next few hours searching for property inspection companies in the *pages jaunes* only to find that like so many surprising things (peanut butter and money orders and until recently, dental floss), they simply did not seem to exist in France.

"How can that be?" I limped around the garden, the pea gravel crunching under my flip flops. "There *must* be somebody that people can turn to here to check out a place – someone they can trust."

Franck snapped his fingers. "*Notaires!*"

"What?"

"Of course there aren't any property inspectors here. Everyone would just ask their notary to do it."

I flopped down on the step beside Franck. "You're right. That has to be it."

Notaires were as essential to life in rural France as country doctors like Le Père Dupont. Families seemed to inherit one from their ancestors and the family *notaire* basically possessed a huge file (or files) of paperwork pertaining to their lives: birth certificates, marriage certificates, the buying and selling of vineyards and houses and more. The files of some Burgundian families spanned back to the 1600s.

My first and only exposure to Franck's family notary – the incompetent Maître Lefebvre – was not felicitous. He was a notorious drinker who cared far more for a good *Gevrey-Chambertin* than doing legal work. The previous summer he had forgotten to get us to fill out several essential forms prior to our wedding. The secretary from Villers-la-Faye's mayor's office called us a week after the ceremony to inform us that, despite the copious amounts of wine and champagne that had been consumed as well as that epic croquembouche that had been gobbled up, as far as the French government was concerned we weren't officially married yet.

"I'll call Maître Lefebvre's office." Franck stood up.

I pulled him back down again. "Not so fast. Remember the shoddy job he did for our wedding?"

This checked him for a moment, but then he shrugged. "But who else could we go to?"

"There have to be other notaries around."

"But none of them know me or my family. Maître Lefebvre may not be the best notary around, but he's *our* notary."

"He's an alcoholic." Franck shrugged as though this was hardly damning enough to justify going elsewhere. "You know, I wonder if Maître Lefebvre has a loose tongue when he drinks?" I continued. "Doesn't he do work for almost everyone in these villages? Are you sure you could trust him not to blab all about the property, especially after a few bottles at lunchtime?"

Franck fiddled with a stray tendril from the wisteria, troubled now. "No," he admitted.

"We need to find someone a bit more anonymous," I pressed my point. "There must be several notaries in Beaune." I hopped up to retrieve the *page jaunes* from the house before Franck could change his mind.

I was right – there were almost as many notaries in Beaune as there were winemakers.

We hopped into the Citroën and drove down through the vineyards to Beaune, finding a parking spot in the shadow of the Notre Dame church. We emerged from the car and began to wander towards the rue Paradis to head down to the Place du Marché, and before we could take four steps we spotted a shiny gold notary seal hanging outside a pair of sleek looking glass doors.

"Look at that!" I said to Franck, who looked as thunderstruck as I felt. A notary's office – and a lovely looking one – right here beside where we had just happened to park our car? I had walked around Notre-Dame hundreds of times and I had never noticed it before. It was as though this notary had materialized out of the ether just for us.

Franck and I hurried over to read the fine print under the golden plaque. *Notaires Associés* – Maître Ange et Maître Perrot.

"Maître Ange? Maître *Ange?* You've got to be kidding me," I muttered to the sky after a few moments of stunned silence. Franck took a step towards the door. It slid open silently to allow us to enter.

The inner sanctum was just as perfect as the outside. At the reception desk sat an impeccably turned out secretary with a gravity-defying *chignon*. Franck, who had a God-given talent for charming secretaries, went up to her and explained our dilemma with regard to the property. We knew we loved it and we wanted to put an offer on it, but we really felt we needed someone like a notary to assure us we weren't making a gigantic mistake.

"*Bien sûr*," she nodded. "That is most prudent. I'm sure Maître Ange will be available to assist you in a few moments."

Franck and I exchanged glances. The waiting room - this was surely the place where the fairytale ended. At Maître Lefebvre's, every visit necessitated a tortuous wait in the purgatory of his airless waiting room filled with sticky, ripped plastic chairs and dog-eared issues of *Paris Match* from the 1980s. The waits seemed to be meticulously timed to test human endurance. Maître Lefebvre's clients were always called in to his office just seconds before they were about to give up and leave.

We edged our way toward the modern chairs and glossy magazines that sat opposite the reception, girding ourselves for a long wait, but before we could even sit down a door to the left of the secretary opened. A man with a head of silver hair and a sharply cut suit ushered us in, shaking our hands warmly and introducing himself as the Maître Ange.

"Pleased to meet you," Franck and I mumbled, both a bit dazed. To be able to see a notary without waiting…this was a completely novel experience. Franck quickly gathered his wits about him and after we had sat down outlined the problem admirably to Maître Ange.

"And what, may I ask, is the selling price?" Le Maître asked after Franck had given a full description of the property.

Franck and I exchanged a worried glance. Was this the moment of truth when Le Maître would snort and say we had just escaped being horrifically ripped off, or that we were idiots not to have bought it for that price already?

"Two hundred and fifty thousand francs," Franck answered. I watched Le Maître, but his composed face revealed nothing. He merely rolled his Mont Blanc between his thumb and his forefinger.

"It does seem perhaps a tad on the high side," he said, non-committal. "Then again, after a long period of stagnation there is renewed interest in these villages and there are a limited number of properties for sale. I believe I must see it before I am able to give you my professional opinion."

Franck winked at me. This is exactly what we had wanted to happen, but we hadn't wanted to come right out and say it.

"How would you like to be… ah… remunerated for your time?" Franck asked delicately.

Le Maître clicked the top of his Mont Blanc pen and bestowed a warm smile on us. "Don't worry about that. We can figure that out later, depending on whether I am able to assist you or not. Now, when shall we arrange for a viewing? I have some availability tomorrow."

Fifteen minutes later the viewing had been set up and we floated out of the notary's office, feeling divinely protected now that we had the Angel Maître on our team.

If only life unfolded like this all the time, faith would be a snap.

CHAPTER 6

The next day, Franck and I found ourselves scuttling back to our hiding spot under the washhouse in Marey. We peered through the round window for a glimpse of either Maître Ange or the realtor.

This time I didn't roll my eyes or complain. I couldn't bear the thought of anyone interfering with us buying the property. In bed that morning Franck and I had already decided that if we saw signs that our Maître Ange approved of the place we would make an offer on the spot to the realtor. I pressed my hot forehead against the cool stone. It was all happening so fast.

Maître Ange arrived perfectly on time in a majestic silver Mercedes that somehow seemed to repel the dust that billowed up from the vineyard roads. Franck and I covertly slid out from the washhouse and crossed the road to greet him. His blue eyes scanned the property.

"*Alors*, this is the place?" he asked.

"*Oui*," Franck said. "The two houses you see here and the two *granges* further down the hill, as well as all the land. It goes all the way down to the vineyards.

Le Maître merely raised his eyebrows and began to walk towards the gate. He unwound the knot of chain and sauntered in as though he owned the place.

"The agent hasn't arrived yet," Franck clarified. "Perhaps we should –"

"I seem to remember you mentioning that the owners had already moved out." Le Maître smiled at us winningly.

"They have," Franck said. "But still…I'm not sure if we have the right - "

"They wouldn't mind prospective buyers such as us looking around, now would they?"

Franck's eyes questioned me and I shrugged. I had argued pretty much the same thing when we first visited the property. Still, it felt more like trespassing when it wasn't my idea.

Le Maître Ange didn't wait around for us to agree or disagree. He strode on, his shining head of silver hair tilted up so he could take in the vast expanse of stone and roof. Franck and I both waited for a sign from him. Nothing seemed to escape his scrutiny. He remained, however, inscrutable.

A honk came from behind us and Franck and I whipped around. Le Maître turned slowly, with one eyebrow cocked to detect the identity of the culprit who dared interrupt his inspection. The agent lurched out of his dusty car, shedding stray pieces of paper and spouting excuses all the way across the lawn to where we stood.

Franck made the introductions. The real estate agent, taking in the gleaming personage of our notary, was struck speechless. Le Maître rubbed his fingers distastefully after shaking hands with the realtor; the realtor blushed, apologetic rather than offended.

"I take it you don't sell a lot of properties around here?" Maître Ange demanded.

"*Non.* This is quite out of my *secteur*. Quite an unusual set of circumstances, actually - "

"*Très bien,*" Le Maître said, neatly nipping what was surely going to be a tedious story in the bud. "I would like to be shown around the property, *s'il vous plait.*"

Trembling, the realtor led us over to the low house first. Even though I was keeping my eye trained on Maître Ange, I couldn't help noticing things that I hadn't noticed before: the huge keyhole in the thick wooden door that led into the kitchen, the marvellous, heavy key to unlock it hanging on the wall by the cooking stove, the smoothness of the wooden banister in the tall house that ran under my palm like silk, not to mention the wild purple clematis growing up towards my little garret up in the far outbuilding. Each new and perfect detail drove home an undeniable fact - my future happiness depended on owning this place.

Maître Ange remained silent during the entire tour, much to our frustration as well as that of the realtor who became more obsequious with every minute that passed. Surely Maître Ange didn't disapprove, I told myself. How could he *possibly* object to such a marvellous property at such a bargain price?

"Do you mind if we confer in private for a moment with our notary?" Franck asked the realtor finally, who remembered a pressing need to fetch something from his car.

"*Alors?*" Franck asked Le Maître as soon as the realtor was out of earshot. "Do you see any problems?"

"Not problems *exactement*," Maître Ange smoothed his hair. "The renovation costs will be extensive. I know for a fact that buyers, particularly first time buyers, tend to grossly underestimate them."

This was surely the truth, especially in our case, but it didn't change the fact that it wasn't what I wanted to hear. An old, almost forgotten, tenacity stirred behind my breastbone.

"I understand your concern about the high renovation costs," I said. "But look at all that property down the hill. If we needed extra money we could subdivide and sell off one or two parcels of land."

Le Maître's eyes turned on me with such a patent look of dislike that I took a step backwards. French professionals such as notaries and doctors were not fans of having their revered judgment questioned. Still, I knew what I had just said wasn't ridiculous. We were beginners, to be sure, but we weren't idiots. I watched, my stomach sinking, as Le Maître struggled to replace his expression of disgust with one of mere exasperation.

There was someone completely different behind that shiny façade, I realized with shock and that someone wasn't inspecting the property for us out of the goodness of his heart.

"I'll have to speak to the agent about that," he said. "You know, find out about the zoning in this village and so forth." He made his way quickly over to the agent, who was still rummaging around the bowels of his car. Le Maître slung his arm around him and pivoted the agent so they were moving away from us, towards the washing house.

"What's he doing?" I hissed to Franck.

"I don't know, but I don't like it."

Our angel now felt more like Lucifer in disguise. We had to act fast. We *had* to get this house. I grabbed Franck's arm. "Let's go ahead and make our offer."

Franck narrowed his eyes at the scheming going on a few feet away. *"Oui."*

"For the asking price?" I said. It wasn't really a question. Franck nodded. Le Maître leaned down and began to whisper into the agent's ear while moving him even farther away from us.

"Tout de suite," Franck added. We moved quickly to break up the worrisome *tête à tête.*

As we neared them, snippets of the promises Le Maître was pouring into our realtor's ear floated over to us. "Already have clients lined up. Switzerland. More than the asking price…just what they are looking for…cut for you…"

My fingers balled into fists.

Franck cleared his throat. The agent jumped.

"We are ready to make an offer," Franck informed him. The agent's face was bright red and, in stark contrast to Le Maître's belligerent countenance, sporting a sheepish expression.

"Quoi?" he spluttered.

"We want to make an offer. *Now."* Franck fixed the pair of them with his famed *oeil noir*, or "black look". "Our offer will match the asking price."

"It will have a time limit of twenty-four hours," I added with an arch look at Le Maître. I wasn't sure why that stipulation had popped into my head, but there was no time to ponder that now.

Le Maître tried to stare me down. "As your advisor, I really do not believe - "

I turned my back to him and smiled at the real estate agent. "Can you please write the offer up?"

Beads of sweat dripped off his earlobes. *"Ici?* Right now?"

I gave an imperious nod.

Le Maître brushed past me and stalked to his Mercedes. Before he got there, however, he turned and shot our realtor a meaningful look. "Call me." He sped off in a cloud of dust. The realtor let out a sound of disbelief at the perfidy of his accomplice.

"What were the two of you plotting?" Franck demanded, his not unimpressive forearms like iron.

"Nothing…*rien du tout*…a simple misunderstanding…it was about another house I have for sale. I have the paper work for this one right here. You are not *truly* ready to sign an offer right now, are you?"

Franck extracted a pen from his back pocket. "Just tell us where to sign."

The realtor clawed a hand through his hair. "If only it were as simple as that! I need to go back to my car and find the paperwork." He gnawed his lip. "But a 24-hour expiry on the offer? *Ce n'est pas possible*! Nobody demands that of the sellers."

"That's not negotiable," I said, waving my hand meaningfully towards the empty space where the notary's car had been parked. "Especially given the circumstances of the last few minutes." It was a desperate tactic, but it was perhaps our only hope of preventing the property from being sold out from underneath us.

The realtor's eyes darted like minnows searching for an escape route, but Franck and I stood elbow to elbow across from him, unyielding.

He sighed and opened his trunk again. "Just let me find the documents. It may take a moment."

I grabbed Franck's hand and squeezed it hard in an attempt to calm myself down. Did he feel as bewildered and angry as I did? Could this really be happening?

Franck chewed on his lip. "I can't believe it," Franck said. "*Les salauds.*" Some urgent whispering came from around the back of the realtor's car. "He's on his cell phone!" Franck hissed. We darted around the open trunk in time to see the realtor gabbing into his cell phone while making frantic gestures with his hands. He was now the color of a ripe aubergine.

"*Merde!*" he gasped as he caught sight of us and hung up without even saying good-bye.

"The paperwork?" I reminded him.

"Turns out I had it in my bag after all." He made a stab at laughter which fell flat with his audience of only Franck and me. "Sorry, phone call with a client," he lied.

"*C'est cela.*" Franck arched a disbelieving brow. "Can we get on with it, please?"

The agent reluctantly slid out a wad of paper from his satchel, shut the trunk to use it as a writing surface, scrawled on the papers here and there, finally shoving them over to us. He pointed to the front sheet.

"You sign here and here. Both of you."

Wasn't there supposed to be more *gravitas* involved in making a written offer? There was, after all, a heck of a lot of money involved. Then again realtors did this kind of thing every day…unless he was just doing this to get rid of us.

Franck read the papers over line by line while the realtor rolled his eyes and rapped his fingers on the hood of his car. Franck then passed them to me. The metal of the car underneath my hip burned through my skirt but I took my time. One of the few useful things I had learned over the past two years was to never skim over a contract.

"You've written nothing here about there being a twenty-four hour limit on the offer," I said once I had scrutinized the last word.

"*Bah*, you are not truly serious about that?"

"*Si*," Franck and I said in unison. I passed the paperwork back.

The realtor scrawled in the twenty-four hour clause and then passed us the pen. I couldn't believe we were making this offer in such a rush. We didn't even know if we would qualify for a mortgage, for heaven's sake. But if that ache in my gut was right about Le Maître*'s* meddling, we had no choice if we wanted our dream property.

I felt exactly the same way about getting this house as I did about finishing my law degree at Oxford. When I walked out of the examination schools after my final exam I was fully expecting that in that very moment all my problems would resolve themselves. Struggle, worry, and doubt would become things of the past.

Franck was there waiting for me as I came down those stairs for the final time, as well as my friends Emmeline and Melanie. They showered me with the traditional confetti and champagne and red carnations. I kept waiting for the click of everything falling into place. Elation was all around me, but it still wasn't *in* me as I had anticipated.

Now I understood. It wasn't getting my law degree that would make everything perfect, it was owning this house.

"You are going to call the sellers right away, *n'est-ce pas?*" Franck's eyes blazed at the realtor.

"*Bien sûr, bien sûr.* I will try them tonight without fail. Are you sure you don't want to extend the deadline by a week or so?"

"*Non*," Franck said. "I will be expecting a call from you tonight after you speak to the owners."

The realtor grimaced, then shook our hands with a perfunctory goodbye and drove off. I watched his shadow as it disappeared in the distance. He was holding his phone to his ear before even rounding the first corner in the village road.

CHAPTER 7

Franck and I spent that evening in his parents' cellar staring at the old-style cord phone in shifts. We gave his family the abridged version of the perfidy of Maître Ange and everyone crept around us, murmuring in hushed tones like someone had died. Mémé brought us plates of her *boeuf bourguignon* to our station on the cellar floor but the succulent meat felt like rubber in my mouth.

We continued to stare at the phone until nine o'clock when Franck finally capitulated and picked up the receiver.

"I'm going to call the realtor," he said, unnecessarily. We both waited, breathless, as he dialled. It rang three times, and then a fourth and a fifth, then clicked over to the realtor's voice mail. Franck was left with no other choice than to leave a curt message that we were still expecting his call.

We finally dragged ourselves up to bed around eleven, and I fell into a restless sleep filled with dreams of scheming, silver-haired notaries.

We woke up early and compared headaches. Franck went over to the *boulangerie* to buy us some *croissants* while I waited by the phone. My skin prickled and my throat seemed to swell with the powerlessness of it all. Maybe I was, in fact, allergic to waiting?

We were just opening the crinkly bag from the *boulangerie* when the phone rang. Franck leapt up and spilled pastries all over the room.

"*Allo?!*" he yelled into the receiver. I was at his side in an instant. It all seemed quite cordial at first - *bonjours* and *ça va biens* and all of that. Then Franck asked, "Have they seen our offer?" and as he listened to the realtor's answer, a storm descended over his face. It couldn't be. This couldn't be happening.

Franck slammed down the receiver without even saying *au revoir* or *merci*.

This was happening.

Franck swore vividly and at length. "He had other offers. Higher offers," he spat. "One in particular from *Switzerland*."

My hand flew up to my throat and I backed up to use the wall behind me for support. We weren't going to get our dream house.

I stomped my foot. If only I could go back and rewind time. I would never have suggested an inspection; we would never have been duped by Maître Ange. I should have trusted our instincts that the property was an amazing deal and gone ahead and bought it right away.

Franck stalked outside and I followed him. I lowered myself down on the front step and cradled my head in my hands. I waited for an onslaught of anxiety to crush me. The dream of the house had distracted me from obsessing about my final examination marks or getting into the Master's program next year at Oxford. My future without the fantasy of our French house seemed bleak indeed yet, bizarrely, the panic didn't come.

The next few days were depressing ones filled with lots of melancholy drives past what I began to think of as our *Paradis Perdu* in Marey-les-Fussey.

Then came our worst drive by, and our last.

As we slowed down in front of our *maison de rêve* (or *maisons*, more accurately, because I clearly have a masochistic bent) we saw the Maître Ange's silver Mercedes ranged alongside an equally gleaming black BMW with a Swiss license plate. We could make out some figures walking down the lawn of the house.

Fury made my heart gallop. "Can we sideswipe their cars?" I asked Franck.

Franck didn't answer, but sped up and did a violent enough U-turn in the dusty parking lot in front of the church to wake up the dead underneath the flagstones.

"*Assez!*" he shouted to the air. "Enough. It's done."

I bit the inside of my cheek. I wanted more than anything to yell at Maître Ange and his fancy Swiss buyers, as well as punch them and maybe throw them down the well. My fists were balled up in my lap, but deep down I knew Franck was right.

Franck pulled the car up in front of his parents' house. He reached over and took my hand in his.

"*Assez?*" he asked, gently.

"*Assez,*" I whispered.

Two days later we dragged ourselves to the Notary's office - not Maître Ange's office, but back to Franck's family notary, Maître Lefebvre, who was too slipshod to be truly devious – to see if any new houses were for sale. Maybe the perfect house was waiting for us at Maître Lefebvre's office. A pinprick of hope pierced the disappointment.

When we outlined what we were looking for to Maître Lefebvre's secretary she blew out between her lips in that French sign of hopelessness and shook her head. She pointed to the corkboard beside her desk where a few dilapidated, overpriced properties were featured on yellowing bits of paper. A brief perusal drove home just how thoroughly we had been shafted by Maître Ange. The Marey property had been a complete steal; it was head and shoulders above all the other ruins and shacks for sale. He had doubtless turned a pretty bit of coin thanks to our naïveté. Without any real hope we spoke to the secretary again about what we were looking for in a property. She rolled her eyes but finally wrote a note on a scrap of paper.

The drive back to Franck's house up into the undulating vineyards of our *Hautes Côtes* was a silent one. There was nothing else we could do except wait for me to get accepted in the Master's program at Oxford in the fall. Our Oxford life would continue behind that shiny blue painted door of our flat on Little Clarendon Street in Jericho. I would spend most of my hours, like I had for the past two years, toiling away behind a pile of dusty casebooks in the law library. Franck and I would hardly ever see each other. Once I had done my articling and paid my lawyerly dues in the form of crazy hours, dull work, and no personal life to speak of, I would become a solicitor in one of the City law firms in London. We would have enough money. We would have steady jobs. Those things would protect us. Maybe we would even be content...

I had chosen law after a blissful four years as an undergraduate English and French Literature student for no other reason than I had been schooled to set my sights on a prestigious career, and Medicine was out of the question for a math-phobic hypochondriac like me. I knew after my first week in Oxford that law was far too analytical and rational for my quirky mind. Quitting, however, equalled failure for me; it simply wasn't an option. Besides, everyone around me - everyone except Franck that is - was as convinced as I was that an Oxford law degree was a sure-fire path to success.

Never once during my two year immersion into the legal world had my soul ever vibrated with excitement like it had over the Marey property. My legal studies were all about safeguarding myself against an uncertain future; the French house was a different kind of dream. It was a leap of faith based on the premise that the future would be fantastic. The dream of owning our *paradis perdu* had changed me. It had given me a taste of something I had forgotten was there.

"Are you nervous about the call?" Franck tucked my hand into his as we meandered through the vineyards between Villers-la-Faye and the village that was perched on the opposite hilltop, Magny-les-Villers. It had been a difficult, aimless week in the aftermath of the swindle and tomorrow my Oxford tutor would be calling me with the marks on my final examinations.

I picked a green grape off the vine and squeezed it between my fingers until I felt a satisfying pop. I needed a 2:1, also called an Upper Second, to gain my definitive admittance into the Master of Law program at Oxford. The disastrous Criminal Law paper I wrote as my very last exam haunted me. If I got a 2:2, or a Lower Second, my application to the Master's program, which had already been conditionally approved, would no longer be automatic. I had no clue what I would do in that instance. I had to get an Upper Second. Even though I couldn't stir up much excitement about returning to our life in Oxford, not getting into the Master's program would essentially be like hitting a dead end in the maze I had taken my entire life to navigate through.

"So?" Franck prompted. "How are you feeling about it?"

Frustrated. Resigned. A bit hopeless even…but I didn't feel it would be fair to admit that to Franck.

The flagstones on the kitchen floor at the house in Marey popped into my head. *That's* what I wanted. I had fallen in love with those flagstones, with the idea of preserving something more steeped in history than any house back home in Canada. I longed to continue my life in a place where generations of other people had lived before me, having Mémé teach me how to make her *mousse au chocolat* in the kitchen and diving under the duvet in that uppermost bedroom with Franck after a long winter's walk through the frosty vineyards…

Franck squeezed my hand. I could tell by the set of his mouth that he was worried about me. Those flagstones were somebody else's property now, I reminded myself. Besides, I owed it to my parents to continue with law. They had paid for the last two years. I had picked my path. If I did indeed get a 2:1 it would be insanity not to continue down it.

"I'll be okay," I answered Franck. He didn't look convinced. We passed the stone cross that marked the entrance to Magny-les-Villers.

"What are the people who live in Magny called?" I asked Franck. I loved how in France the inhabitants of the biggest city to the smallest hamlet had a name for themselves, from *Parisiens* (Paris) to *Nuitons* (Nuits-Saint-Georges) to *Buissoniers* (Buisson).

"*Magnotins,*" Franck said, pronouncing the word with a soft "g". "The women are called *Magnotines.*"

"I like that. It has a medieval ring to it."

We made our way past the stone house of the *maître d'école* who had taught Franck, Franck's sister Stéphanie, and their little brother Emmanuel-Marie at the village school. His garden was taken over by wild hollyhocks, many taller than Franck. Next was the communal well where an old red rose climbed up and over the crumbling stone wall behind. The road wound down in front of the village church. It was a small, Roman affair like the one on Marey. It glowed ochre in the late afternoon sunlight.

"Have I ever brought you here before?" Franck asked me.

I shook my head. It had been Franck who had come to Burgundy on his own and toured every single church in Villers and the surrounding villages, looking for the perfect one for us to get married in. I had stayed back at Oxford, chained to the casebooks in the law library.

"I don't know if I ever told you this, but this church was actually my first choice for our wedding."

"What happened?"

"It was booked for a christening so I booked the one in Marey instead."

The wooden door, intricately carved and only made more beautiful by the scars of the centuries, was fitted with one of the most ancient iron locking mechanisms I had ever seen. The metal swirled this way and that, and the notched keyhole could undoubtedly only be opened by a mammoth key. Franck turned the handle and pushed open the door.

The church was cool and seemed almost pitch black until my eyes began to adjust to the softly coloured light that filtered through the stain-glass windows. On the floor were massive stones carved with names and dates in old French. The biggest ones led up to an austere little nave of pale stones behind a wooden altar.

To the left of the door stood a stone basin with a pool of water at the bottom. Franck dipped his fingers in it and crossed himself with the ease of someone who had been baptized, confirmed, and communed a Catholic. Envy prickled at my fingertips.

I had never had a religion. Well, that was not technically true - I had been baptized in an Anglican ceremony and to this day I'm not really sure why except that my cousin was also baptized then. Perhaps the church was running a two for one deal. It was definitely odd considering that my family and most of our friends considered organized religion suspicious at best. My father never failed to regale us with tales of the hypocrisy of churchgoers, such as the local bishop who bet the entire diocese's money on racehorses and lost, the Catholic priest who was found to have a wife and children stashed away in Vancouver, and the minister who fiddled with the altar boys.

As a result, I felt like an interloper in every church I entered. There was something about this church, though, that made me want to believe in God the same way I had believed in Santa Claus during those brief but magical years of early childhood.

I didn't discover the truth about Santa Claus until I was eleven, rather late in the scheme of things. I had begun to notice that Santa and my mother had remarkably similar handwriting and often used the same wrapping paper. That morning I bounced into my parents' bed at the ungodly hour of five o'clock and began pestering my mother.

"Is it really Santa who puts the presents under the tree or is it you?"

"What do you think?" she asked me, groggy.

"I think it might be you. Is it?" I wanted more than anything for her to tell me I was wrong.

"Yes."

That single word turned my world of magic into a gray, rational planet where everything had an explanation. An aching void remained.

"*Viens.*" Franck pulled me over to one of the wooden benches near the front. The seats were polished and scarred with centuries of use. He sat me down, and pointed to the inscription carved deep into the wood in front of me. "Look at that."

"F. Germain," I read, surprised. "Was that carved in there for your ancestors?"

He shrugged. "I don't think so but who knows, really? If it is, it's farther back than even Mémé can remember. Strange though, isn't it?"

But it wasn't really. Of course Franck's name was carved in an old church bench. It had always been clear to Franck, and to me, that he was protected by a higher power. Franck was convinced that no matter what stupid things he did in life, like driving his friend's *mobilette* under a truck on the highway when he was fourteen, he was shielded from harm. How I envied that conviction.

The fact that my husband didn't agree with the Pope's position on birth control or gay marriage or a myriad of other things didn't shake his faith one iota. Some of his best memories of his youth came from his stint as an altar boy. It was the best way to meet new girls from other villages, he had explained to me, not to mention there was never a lack of excellent sacramental wine to enjoy. I envied his freedom to take what he wanted from his religion and leave the rest.

Beside me, Franck bowed his head and closed his eyes. I had become used to his praying whenever we were in a church. I could almost see the young altar boy he had been, complete with an angelic white robe and a heavy wooden cross the size of a *pain au chocolat* around his neck, transposed onto the man he was now.

Part of me wanted to pray for strength while I waited for tomorrow's phone call. Instead I stared at the statue of the Virgin Mary in the stone alcove in front of us. Much of her paint had worn off, but her eyes were still visible. The carver had made them very kind. They were the eyes of someone I wanted to talk to – the eyes of someone who wouldn't laugh at the grief I felt over losing the house in Marey or the ridiculousness of someone as privileged as me drowning in anxiety much of the time. Tears filled my eyes. Without opening my mouth or closing my eyes, I found my thoughts projecting out to her.

I know you're the Virgin Mary and you probably have better things to worry about, like that little Baby Jesus in your arms for example, but I need help. I have been so miserable over the past few months – no, truthfully, over the past two years. I know I must be on the right path but could you please make me feel happier on it? The expression in her eyes seemed to change in the shadows, becoming even more compassionate as she took in every one of my tormented thoughts. *Can you please make this horrible fear that makes me feel like sometimes I can't even take one more breath, and that is eating away at who I am, disappear? Could you give me a sign to let me know that things are going to get better, that I will one day start to feel happy with my life and what I'm doing? I don't know what's wrong with me that I am so ungrateful. Help me. Show me the way. Je t'en supplie.*

I could have sworn she blinked slowly in response. I felt calmer than I had in a long time. It made no sense, of course, but I still couldn't break away from the understanding in her eyes.

Franck's hand slipped into mine and we waited for a few moments more, neither of us wanting to break the peace that seemed to flow around us both. We didn't speak until we had made our way back out into the sunshine. I closed the carved wooden door behind us feeling as though I was also closing it on my troubles; I had left them inside in excellent hands.

I blinked until the peeling white shutters of the ramshackle house across the street came into focus.

"What did you pray for?" I asked Franck. We began walking back up the hill towards the vineyards and Villers-la-Faye. "Or is it like a wish and if you say it won't come true?"

"I prayed that you hear what you want to hear when the phone call comes tomorrow."

A lump of gratitude stuck in my throat. His prayer had been for me.

"I love you," I reached up to kiss him.

Getting what I wanted would be wonderful, of course. The only thing better, like I had confided in the Virgin, was to get what I needed.

CHAPTER 8

The lists of finals marks were being posted outside the Examination Schools in Oxford's High Street. I knew that, like every year, a mob of students, armed with champagne bottles, were clamoring over one another to get a glimpse of their grade. They were desperate, like I was, to find out those two little numbers that possessed the power to radically alter their future for better or for worse. A 1:1, or "First", would pave the way for money, glory, and fame. A 2:1, or "Upper Second", earned respect, whereas, a 2:2, or "Lower Second", was a mark that could dog a person's steps until their dying day in England.

After learning the verdict of their Oxford career the students would careen off to The Turf or The Bear to celebrate or drown their sorrows over champagne and pints. As for me, I was sitting at Franck's kitchen table, watching the clock for the scheduled time when I needed to go upstairs into Franck's bedroom and await the phone call from my tutor, the taciturn Mr. Partridge. He had promised to phone me with my grades as soon as he returned to college from the Examination Schools. He was an unusually young tutor and quivered with ambition like a plucked violin string. It was even more stressful a day for him than it was for his students. He wanted to collect as many Firsts and Upper Seconds among his students as possible. This reflected glory could push him up the byzantine levels of status amongst Oxford academics. Bad results would be like hitting a snake in Snakes and Ladders; one tended to slither down much faster than one climbed up.

Mr. Partridge had been helping me with my application to the

Master's program, but he had already made clear to me that this wasn't solely out of the goodness of his heart.

"It looks good for me to have my students continue on in the Master's program here," he had informed me when I asked him to write me a letter of reference. He had offered to review my whole application, made me make a bunch of changes, and had mentioned the Master's program almost every time he saw me during my last year of law school, both as an encouragement and a threat.

I was swirling the final drops of my *café au lait* in my bowl when the bell to the front gate rang. Franck's mother went out, flustered and still in her dressing gown, to see who was there. Shortly after, she returned to the kitchen followed by a tiny old man whose spine was so crooked that he shuffled along almost bent in two.

Franck made the introductions. This was the *Père Bard*, the ninety and something year old village priest who uncannily resembled a gnome and who had taught Franck and several generations of village children how to fly a kite as well as how to say their "*Je Vous Salue Maries*". *Père Bard* didn't have the reputation of being very interested in his adult parishioners. His true calling was the children of his parish, but not in the way that has sadly become assumed of priests. It was more that he had always retained his own childlike spirit and wanted to surround himself with that energy. He and the village children put on convoluted and tortuously long plays for the parents, travelled down South to the Spanish border on the train to volunteer at Lourdes, and took long walks on *Les Chaumes* searching for an *orchis*, a rare orchid that grew wild in the *Hautes-Côtes*.

The *Père Bard* shook my hand and settled himself down in the chair opposite me. He refused Michèle's offer to divest himself of his voluminous black cape which must have been stifling in the July heat. We all watched him as he carefully rested his battered cane against the kitchen table, waiting for him to inform us of the purpose of this visitation. He looked back at us with an amused glitter in his eyes.

"*Alors*, how have you been keeping, *Mon Père*?" André finally asked.

"I come for toilet paper rolls."

Michèle, who had grown up around the *Père Bard*, did not seem particularly surprised by this pronouncement. "Empty ones?" she asked.

"*Oui*. As many as you have. I've been making dolls with the children and we've run out. So you see, I have no choice but to come begging."

He foraged around in his black cape and drew out a toilet paper roll with twigs sticking out of it for arms and silver tinsel hanging down in a fringe around the top for hair. "Do you see? These are what we are going to make. Isn't she lovely?" He danced the toilet paper roll doll across the air as he hummed a jaunty little tune. I was riveted.

"I'm not sure I have very many for you, but I'll see what I can find," Michèle warned as she got up to look.

He placed the doll down tenderly on the table and tapped his fingers on the polished wood. "Now then, how are you all today?" he asked Franck and André and myself. "As for me, I quite fancy a coffee. Am I the only one?"

"Of course!" André leapt up and Franck followed him. "We'll go and make a pot right away."

Le Père watched them go, then beckoned me closer with a crooked finger.

"What do you think of my dolls?" he whispered once I had leaned in.

"Very nice," I said. "The children will have fun with them."

"Yes." He beamed at me with a mostly toothless smile, picked up the doll and danced it around some more. He stopped suddenly and fixed me with translucent blue eyes. "I always did believe, you know, that God has created all of this because he wants us to have fun." He twirled his hand around, encompassing the kitchen table, the house, the whole world. He began to hum again as his words sunk into me like pebbles thrown in a river.

God put us here to have *fun*? What about hard work and not quitting and climbing the career ladder? I tried to think of the last time I had done something just because it was fun. Nothing came to mind. Nothing at all.

Le Père Bard thrust the doll into my hand. "I'd like to see you try," he said. I made a half-hearted attempt at jerking the doll through the air. He rolled his eyes. "It doesn't work if you don't *sing*."

I began to hum and then encouraged by his nods, broke into a rollicking chorus of row-row-row your boat while flitting the doll around above my head.

"Very nice." He cut me off just as I was getting into the swing of things and gestured at me to hand the doll back. "I must hurry back, you know. Perhaps you should go and check on how they are coming along with the toilet paper rolls and my *café*."

Just then Michèle came back into the room. "I could only find three," she handed them to him and he tucked them somewhere under the folds of his cape.

"Three is marvellous." He winked up at her. "*En plus*, I still get a free coffee."

Franck glanced at the clock just after we waved au revoir to the *Père Bard*.

"Let's go upstairs," he said. "I'll set the phone up for you in the bedroom." I checked my watch. Mr. Partridge would be calling in about ten minutes' time. I nodded and headed towards the stairs like a condemned person heads towards the scaffold.

Up in Franck's bedroom he set up the phone on the bedside table using a huge red extension cord. "This way you can lie on the bed and watch the clouds while you're waiting," he patted the mattress. "Do you want me to stay here with you?"

"Stay with me until the call comes," I said. "I think I need to be alone after that."

I lay back on the bed and Franck lay down beside me. I reached over and grasped his hand. We lay like that, side-by-side for I don't know how many minutes; I saw a dragon float by in the rectangle of blue sky above us, then a Citroën Deux Chevaux, and then…

A shrill ring shattered the peace. Annoyance reared up in my chest, but it was quickly overtaken by the urge to throw up. I gave myself a shake and picked up the receiver.

"*Bonjour.*"

I must have sounded convincing as Mr. Partridge paused for a few seconds, then tried to ask for me in French. Thinking of the *Père Bard*, I listened to my suave tutor butcher the French language with unholy appreciation.

"This is Laura," I admitted, after he was done. "Hello."

Franck blew me a kiss and ducked out the doorway.

"It was you " The starch had already returned to Mr. Partridge's voice. "I just returned from the Examination Schools." He waited. I had forgotten how the British could be sadists, or maybe this was revenge for the French thing. Was he going to make me beg for them?

My heart pounded in my chest but I waited.

"There is some good news and some bad news. Which do you want first?" Bad news. It must have been that Criminal Law paper. How bad was bad? Had it wrecked my chances of getting into the Master's program? "Where do you want me to start?"

"Good news," I said.

"You were awarded a 2:1 overall." My shoulders dropped down a notch. There! I had done it – acquitted myself well with a 2:1, a perfectly honorable grade. It also meant I was in for the Master's program. I waited for a swoop of relief, but it didn't come right away. Where was the room for the bad news?

"But?" I prompted.

"There was a fairly disappointing mark on your Criminal paper. A beta minus. What happened?"

It all came rushing back. Criminal Law had been my last paper. I had pushed myself as far as I could be pushed. What happened was that my stomach was so upset from the stress that I vomited blood on the morning of that final exam. What had happened was that I felt dizzy, as though I was on the verge of passing out. What had happened was that I couldn't seem to get enough air in my lungs no matter how much I gasped. That is what had happened, but I couldn't say any of that to Mr. Partridge.

"It was my last paper," I said, simply. I had been well trained not to complain to an Oxford tutor about the stress of finals. They saw it every year and I deserved no different treatment than the rest. If everyone else could cope, I should be able to as well. We were all expected to suck it up and soldier on.

"Luckily, most people won't have to know about your Criminal Law paper."

He meant it was shameful, something to be ferreted away at all costs because marks were the religion of Oxford. It was a race and just like that single asphalt lane in front of a sprinter, the world narrowed down so that the only reality you could comprehend was that one tunnel that lay out in front of you.

"Okay," I said. I felt the queasy lie settle in my stomach.

"Now for the bad news."

"I thought the Criminal paper was the bad news?"

"Not exactly. It's about the Master's program."

"But the cut off is a 2:1. You just told me I received a 2:1…"

Mr. Partridge cleared his throat. "There are an unusually high number of candidates for next year. As a consequence, they're changing the entrance requirements."

"But I've already been offered a provisional acceptance based on getting a 2:1," my voice came out shrill. I had pretty much sold my soul to complete my end of the bargain, how dare they renege on the deal?

"True. They do, however, have the right to change the requirements even after a provisional acceptance has been offered. It's in the small print. Remember that you are dealing with lawyers. They are very good at small print." He laughed at his own joke.

I didn't join in. "So they won't let me in now? Is that it?"

"Don't jump to conclusions yet. I have thought out a plan of attack. We may have to fight for it, but I believe our chances are excellent. I will write a letter supporting your candidature, and let it be known that you were taught Criminal Law by an inexperienced teacher-"

"My mark wasn't my teacher's fault. I was the one who bombed that exam."

"That approach won't serve us," Mr. Partridge replied. "I will explain that your teacher's lack of competency is the reason for that atypically low mark." Mr. Partridge made a funny little sound of satisfaction, a sound someone would make without realizing it as they preened themselves in the mirror. "With that and my recommendation, I am sure they will find a place for you."

The phone line went silent. I couldn't believe how quickly he would torpedo my teacher's reputation just for the glory of getting one more student into the Master's program. He was waiting for a thank you, I realized, and my reiteration that, as any sane Oxford student would say, I wanted a spot in the coveted Master's program more than life itself. I opened my mouth but no words came out.

"They will want to interview you," he added. "You must return to Oxford immediately."

I twisted the black phone cord around my wrist. Back to Oxford?

Now?

"Are you still on the line Laura?"

Stone walls flashed through my mind beside polished flagstones and a centuries old wooden statue of the Virgin Mary.

"*Non*," I whispered.

"I beg your pardon?"

"*Non*." It came out in French again, louder this time, and sounded like the response of an impetuous five-year-old who had just been ordered to give back the *bonbon* she had stolen from her brother.

"But I can hear you. You must still be on the line."

"I meant the Master's program."

A pause of disbelief. "You mustn't worry about it not being fair tactics, you know. That is simply the way - "

"No!" It came out in clear English this time and louder still. We were both stunned into silence for a few seconds. He spoke first.

"I simply don't understand," he admitted, peevish.

"I...I appreciate your offer," I stumbled over my words. "I really do. It's just that...maybe that Criminal paper is a sign that I'm not meant to do the Master's program after all."

"Nonsense! You mustn't undersell yourself. You must know by now that one thing we value above all at Oxford is self-confidence. It is imperative that you believe in yourself, Laura. You will never get ahead otherwise."

Did I still want to get ahead, Oxford style? That was the question. What I really wanted was to watch the clouds float by and make toilet paper roll dolls and wake up in my own little house in France.

"I'm not certain I want to get ahead anymore," I said.

I knew that in his Oxford office Mr. Partridge was shaking his head in disbelief.

"Laura," he began, his voice soothing now. "I believe that perhaps the pressure has affected your judgment. I suggest that you take a day or two to think things over. Not any longer than that, mind. If we are to be successful we must start campaigning as soon as possible."

Telling an Oxford student that the pressure had got to them was just about the worst form of insult. A month ago I would have done almost anything to prove Mr. Partridge wrong, but now...

"Thank you for the offer," I said. "I appreciate your efforts. Truly. But I believe I'm coming to the conclusion that perhaps law isn't for me after all."

"Did you get accepted to a Master's program somewhere else?" he demanded.

"I didn't even apply anywhere else."

"Then what on earth are you going to do?"

I turned this question over in my mind for a good while. "I have no idea," I said, at last. Part of me vibrated in panic while the other half soared with relief.

Mr. Partridge didn't say anything for a moment. I knew how bizarre my answer sounded to someone inside the Oxford universe, a place where every step up was minutely planned and anticipated, where a choice that turned its back on academic or professional achievement was unthinkable.

"Are you absolutely certain you don't want to take a few days to think this over?" His voice had now taken on the hushed, soothing quality I'd heard being used with mental patients.

This was my last chance to go back to my old life. From day one though, I had hated studying law and I knew now with every cell in my body that I would always hate studying law. There were so many other things I had discovered I loved however - smooth wooden banisters running under my palm and old stone wells. Maybe we had lost our paradise in Marey, but that dream had allowed me to realize what I loved and, more importantly, what I did not.

"I'm sure," I said.

CHAPTER 9

I was still sitting with the phone cord twisted around my wrist when Franck crept back into the room.

"Bad news?"

I wasn't quite sure how to answer. Was it bad news? I wasn't sorry so much as stunned.

"I got a 2:1," I said.

"That's what you wanted, right?" Franck asked, unsure. "Isn't that a good mark?"

How asinine to have spent two years sacrificing everything just to be awarded a number that meant nothing in the real world.

"It's what I wanted. We won't be going back to Oxford though." I peered up into Franck's face, expecting shock and disapproval, but I only saw a huge smile. "I told Mr. Partridge I didn't want to do the Master's program after all. I have no idea what we're going to do next," I admitted.

Franck pulled me up from the bed and gathered me in his arms. I nestled my head under his chin and inhaled his familiar smell of apples and freshly cut wood. "That is the best news I have heard in a long time." He kissed my forehead and then that tender spot behind my earlobe. "I happen to be good friends with the unknown. *Allons*, I have a chilled bottle waiting for us downstairs."

In the days that followed I often felt that sickening feeling of teetering on the edge of a cliff with imminent disaster directly below. I had absolutely no idea how Franck and I were going to earn enough money to eat and have a roof over our heads, let alone figure out what we really enjoyed doing in life. This, however, was alleviated by moments of untrammelled glee that I associated with being in elementary school and hearing on the radio that it was a snow day.

Franck didn't know any better than I did what the future held; this didn't bother him in the slightest. He was confident that, thanks to his capacity for hard work and the protection of his guardian angels, we would thrive. Still, despite my worries, that "*non*" during my phone call with Mr. Partridge had come from somewhere deep inside me - a place that I hadn't listened to in a very long time.

Franck and I slowly came to the decision to move back to Vancouver to figure things out, closer to my family and a better job market than Burgundy. We couldn't stay *chez Germain* indefinitely if we were going to build our own life.

"If only we'd got that house," Franck often said, with more wistfulness now than bitterness.

"If we had got the house, we'd have a huge mortgage to pay, tons of repairs to do, and no money to do it with," I reminded him. Of course, part of me lusted for that lost project just as much as Franck. Still, it had taught me to dream again and nobody – not even a scheming notary or rich buyers from Switzerland - could take that away from me.

I finally bought our airline tickets back to Canada. I also did my best to placate my family by telling them I was going to try to qualify as a lawyer in Vancouver. It wasn't dishonest, really. Most of the time I believed that I would have no choice but to go that route. How long could I play hooky for, after all?

Then just five days before we were scheduled to leave for Vancouver, a short scribbled note arrived from Franck's family notary. The handwriting was appalling. Franck and I sat on the warm stone steps to the kitchen with André hovering behind us, squinting at the note in an attempt to decipher the Maître Lefebvre's hieroglyphics.

"I think that this says '*maison*.'" André pointed to one of the more legible scrawls.

"And that looks like the number eighteen written in Roman numerals," Franck said.

"Doesn't that say 'Magny'"? I asked them, pointing to another word.

Mémé came out and swatted us off the steps with her dishtowel. She had no patience for loungers in her path. She had just finished making about thirty or so quiches and needed to take them across to the freezer in the *grange*.

"What's that in your hand?" she demanded of Franck.

"We're not quite sure," Franck said. "It's from Maître Lefebvre." She plucked it out of Franck's hand and scanned it with her habitual authority.

"Charming Eighteenth Century Village house located in the centre of Magny-les-Villers," she read, without pausing. "Wonderful view on the Roman church across the street and exquisite oak beams in attic. Call for further information." She passed the note back to Franck and marched across the gravel courtyard with her bags of quiches.

"How could you read that?" Franck called after her.

She emerged from the barn a few seconds later, mid-shrug. "His writing is exactly the same as his father's. His father wrote my divorce settlement." She snapped her dishtowel at an errant wasp, dismissing any further questions on that subject.

Franck touched my arm. "His office must be closed now, but do you want to go to Magny and see if we can find the house he's talking about?"

I grimaced. My heart had been broken over the property in Marey. I couldn't picture wanting to buy any other house for several months, maybe years, at least.

His touch turned into a light caress. "It's not far for us to go. It would be a nice walk."

"It's probably already sold," I said.

"I doubt it," Mémé said. "Why would he bother sending you the note otherwise? I don't think Le Maître would make such an effort unless he really needed to get rid of something."

I sighed, realizing that Franck was not going to give up until he had seen the house, one way or another. "There's no point in going to Magny today. We probably wouldn't even be able to tell which house he is talking about. Go ahead and call him tomorrow morning to make an appointment, just to satisfy your curiosity. Don't forget we're leaving in five days, though."

Franck scanned the note again. "I have a good feeling about this."

I had no feelings about it at all. I wasn't ready to fall in love again.

The next morning, Franck had called Le Maître before I had even crawled out from under our duvet. Of course Franck urged the secretary to make the appointment as soon as possible, but apparently it was unthinkable for Le Maître to meet us before three o'clock that afternoon.

Leaving for the scheduled rendezvous, I felt as cynical as a jaded divorcée in the lead up to a blind date. By three o'clock the temperature was hovering around forty degrees Celsius. Standing in the sun, even for a few seconds in my light dress, gave me the impression I was being baked alive. We took shelter in the alcove's shade of the little Roman church where I had poured my heart out to the Virgin Mary statue just days before. I didn't even spare a cursory glance around me to try and figure out which of the six or so village houses we would be touring. It didn't really matter; I was determined to be unimpressed.

Half an hour later Le Maître came roaring up in his Renault and took out two of the scarlet rose bushes planted alongside the church in his attempt to park. Le Maître emerged, shrugged an apology to the flattened flowers, and made his way over to us. We stood up and he shook our hands.

"Madame, Monsieur Germain," he intoned with an air of unshakable professionalism that was undermined by the wine vapors which emanated from his pores.

"*Bonjour, Maître*," Franck said. "Which house will we be visiting?"

Le Maître waved vaguely toward the three houses on the opposite side of the road. "That one." He patted his pockets. "*Mon Dieu*, where are the keys?" This was annoying but it also made me less wary. It didn't appear that, unlike Maître Ange, Maître Lefebvre could organize a scam even if he wanted to. Franck and I exchanged a look and retreated to the cool of the nave once more.

After five minutes of searching every pocket and tuck in his clothing as well as emptying out the glove compartment of his car, Le Maître made an irate call to his *secrétaire*. He demanded what she could have possibly done with the keys to the house. It was clear from the vastly entertaining string of swear words that followed this brief exchange that she basically told him to go to hell.

Just when I was sure that the visit was not going to happen, a huge bundle of long, iron keys was extracted from some hidden rear pocket of Le Maître's pants. It was incredible that he could have missed them in his body search. The wine consumption at lunch must have been prodigious indeed.

Le Maître triumphantly dangled the key ring in front of us. I had always loved old keys, and these ones were spectacular, but that didn't mean I wanted the house that went with them. I had to keep a clear mind.

He beckoned us across the street and we followed him underneath a little archway of stone, which the enamel plaque on the crumbling plaster wall designated as the "Passage Saint-Martin". Le Maître veered to the right and began to climb a flight of large stone stairs, each one about seven feet wide.

Mid-climb Franck stopped in his tracks and I bumped into his back. "These have to be from the local quarry," he said, pointing down at the ripples of pink and ochre that ran through the stone. Uh oh. His grandfather (the fabled Pépé Georges who could sulk for days and who was now one of Franck's squad of Guardian Angels) had worked all his life in the local quarry; Franck had a soft spot for anything that came from there.

The first door the Maître unlocked was a run-of-the-mill metal door, painted an unedifying shade of gray. I peeked around Franck and was satisfied to see the walls of the veranda itself were unpainted concrete. Ugly. The veranda was roofed with pieces of glass that magnified the heat. I was sure I was going to keel over while Le Maître tried several keys unsuccessfully.

When the door finally swung open we all surged forward to get into the relative cool of the house. I turned to shut the door behind me to keep out the heat and my hand fell on one of the most arcane and complicated latching mechanisms I had ever seen on a door. My eyes travelled higher. The door itself was intricately carved wood that reminded me of the door of the church across the street. Inserted in it was a black metal design of flowers.

Franck had a thing for stone. I had a thing for keys, locks, and doors.

As I penetrated further into the dark interior of the house my nostrils were assaulted by the stench of mothballs and mildew. It took a good minute or two for my pupils to dilate, but when they did I could make out the wallpaper - a fake rattan pattern of greens and yellows in the hallway that gave way to a leaf and flower explosion of browns, greens, and oranges in the living room beyond.

"It reminds me of my grandmother's house when I was little,' Franck commented, wistfully.

"It's hideous," I said, loud enough for Le Maître to hear.

Le Maître waltzed into what looked like a tiny kitchen, the walls of which were papered in green ivy.

"It is hideous," he agreed. "But look at this view." He swung open the shutters, and I saw from the flaking white paint that we were in the house I had noticed after emerging from the church following my stream-of-consciousness conversation with the Virgin Mary statue. He opened the single pane windows. "*Voilà!*" he exclaimed, and drew back so we could have a look.

Franck gave me a gentle nudge towards the open window. Because the house was up that flight of stone stairs from the street level, the windows were level with the church. It was an intriguing perspective. I paused to admire its entranceway of old oak beams and square stones and its long, thin minion window. My eyes travelled up the small but elegant spire that was topped with a metal rooster.

All we would have to do to get the weather forecast was look out the kitchen window in the morning over our *café au lait* and check if the rooster's head or tail feathers were facing south. Something familiar fluttered under my breastbone. We're not going to buy this house, I reminded myself, so there was no point in daydreaming about eating breakfast here. We were going back to Canada in five days.

"Hey!" I exclaimed, despite myself. "I can see Stéphanie and Thierry's roof from here."

Franck came over and I felt his hand brush the small of my back. "We didn't have any family in Marey," he said.

I turned my back on the view and inspected the kitchen. The view was just about the only thing it had going for it. The room was tiny and half shoehorned under the stairs that led to the attic. A massive white ceramic sink took up at least a third of the wall which left space for only a small fridge and stove to be placed under the crooked line of the stairs.

"*C'est très petit*...small," I was going to say, but was stopped by a thunk as Le Maître clonked his head on the very low door jam.

"*Merde! Fichu* ancient doorways!" His brows drew in with regret at his not very strategic outburst, but he added in a petulant tone, "That door jamb should have been raised long ago."

He pointed at the simple latch that looked as though it had been made of beaten metal. "Look at that! That must have been hand beaten by the village ironmonger a few hundred years ago. I don't believe they have even bothered to change the door since then."

Franck caught my eye and cocked a brow. He followed Le Maître circumspectly into the next room, leaving me alone in the kitchen.

As soon as they were gone I ran my finger over the cool beaten metal of the massive latch. I pictured the village ironmonger bent over his fire several hundred years before, banging it into shape. Sweat would have dripped from his face into the open fire, filling his low ceilinged workshop with steam. I was scandalized at the thought of anyone changing or modernizing this piece of history. I closed the door reverently and worked the latch. It still slid into place perfectly.

Now that the door was closed, I noticed the hinges. I'd never seen such marvellous things, beaten in a curlicue design and each about seven inches long. They were like something out of a medieval castle. I didn't want the rest of the house, I told myself as I opened the door again, I just wanted this kitchen door and its hardware...and the front door too…and maybe those stone stairs for Franck…

I joined Franck and Le Maître in the living room which was lit by a solitary bulb on the ceiling. I could only just make out the walls – a riot of orange and brown which made me feel less in danger of falling for the house. Franck was over by the window on the far wall, trying to get it open. He had managed to open the shutters just as I joined him and we took in the view over the humble Roman church. Its effect was more seductive for me than any view over a Gothic cathedral. Something in that church had given me a taste of peace. It was the same thing that had made me talk – dare I say pray? – to the Virgin Mary. I had never prayed in any other church before in my life. I tore myself away from the view to glance around the living room again. It didn't matter. We could not buy a house before we left, especially one with wallpaper this nauseating.

Just then my eyes alighted on the massive stone fireplace that took up almost half of the back wall. Franck had noticed it too; he walked over and stood inside it without hitting his head. He ran his index finger over a thick ribbon of ochre rippling through the roughly hewn stone.

"This is incredible," he said. "Not only is it typically Burgundian, but I do believe we could roast an entire cow in here."

Le Maître was inspecting a small cupboard door inset into the wall to the right of the fireplace. Its latch and hinges were stunning, obviously the handiwork of the same ironmonger who had fashioned the latches and hinges of the kitchen door several hundred years before.

"That's a strange place to have a cupboard," I said, drawing in for a closer inspection.

Le Maître smiled at me. "Put your head inside."

I hesitated but Le Maître looked so amused that curiosity got the better of me. I slid open the beautiful iron latch. Maybe a hidden treasure? A blast of cool air hit my face; as my eyes adjusted to the darkness I could make out that the walls of the long hole inside were made up of huge blocks of stone. I couldn't resist reaching my hand out and feeling the surface of the stone which was polished smooth with use and time.

Le Maître quizzed. "Can you guess what it is?"

I removed my head. "No idea."

"I'll give you a clue. Almost every house used to have one but now they are increasingly rare. They let the cold in, *vous voyez*, so most of them have been filled in and drywalled up. "Still no idea?"

I thought for a moment. "Nope."

Le Maître clicked his tongue at my answer. "It's a *réfrigérateur*!"

A fridge? "Really?"

"*Bien sûr*! How do you think people kept their perishable food cold before electricity? See how it is so deep? It can hold a lot of cheese."

I stuck my head back in again. It was amazingly cool within the slabs of stone, even on a scorching summer day such as this. And with that, Franck and I exchanged glances. Saying *non* to Mr. Partridge and now falling in love with another house. Maybe I was fickle after all.

About half an hour later, after touring the bedrooms, the attic and the cellars, we took our leave of Le Maître.

"What did you think?" he tried to feel us out as he opened his car door.

Franck pursed his lips disdainfully. "It would need a lot of work."

Le Maître squinted back toward the peeling white shutters and sighed. "*Oui*, but it could have much charm. The owners have had it listed with me for quite some time, but now they are talking of bringing in the real estate agents." He spat out these last three words as if they were poison.

A few years ago real estate agents were all but unheard of in France. Notaries, and only notaries, handled all real estate transactions; people sold all their vines and houses and pig sheds through the very same notaries that their family had been using for centuries. During the past few years though real estate agents had arrived on the scene and multiplied like rabbits. They were viewed by many as just another symptom of the "Americanisation" of France. Particularly, *bien sûr*, by the notaries.

His words had their desired effect, nevertheless. The owners were talking about listing the house? That meant that it could be splashed over the real estate ads in a matter of days. That meant that we could have a second house stolen out from under our noses. But wait…no…we didn't want this house. This was all happening too late. The timing was all wrong. We were leaving in five days.

I opened my mouth to say something, but Franck must have read my expression. He stilled my words with the briefest touch on the nape of my neck and said to Maître Lefebvre, "We'll get back to you."

Back at Franck's house we sat under the wisteria and contemplated our options over a kir. Franck leaned back on his chair against the warm stone of his parents' barn. We each waited for the other to speak first.

As much as the Marey property was grandiose and majestic, the house across from the church in Magny was humble. It consisted of the veranda, the entranceway, the tiny under-the-stairs kitchen, the living room with the stone fireplace and the cheese fridge, a bathroom, a separate WC, or "water closet" (as in most French houses) and two bedrooms with crooked walls and lovely oak floors. There was also the attic that we visited by taking the crooked set of wooden stairs. I wasn't brave enough to step out on to the dodgy looking floor boards but from the top of the stairs I could make out the gorgeous oak beams in the attic gloom, complete with huge oak pegs that had been used instead of nails to stick them all together. If we ever redid that space, it could be spectacular.

"I think it could work," I said, finally taking the plunge.

Franck's chair clunked forward on the pea gravel. "*Vraiment?*"

I chewed my lip. "It's a lot smaller than the property in Marey, but maybe that's a good thing. It means less money, less risk…we'll be able to keep things more flexible."

"Do you really think so?"

"*Pourquoi pas?*"

CHAPTER 10

The next morning, breakfast wasn't even cleared before we whipped out a pad of paper and a calculator. This time, we wouldn't be involving any additional notaries besides our own *maître* who, as representative of both the buyer and seller, had every motivation to get the deal done.

"What was the asking price again?' I asked. I had never been able to wrap my mind around math in the same way I had say, Shakespeare. *Francs* had always flustered me. They had to be divided by a figure with five digits after the decimal point to get the equivalent amount in dollars.

Mémé, who had been kneading bread, leaned over Franck's shoulder and read the confused and poorly photocopied property information sheet that Le Maître had handed to us as an afterthought after showing us the house in Magny.

"I can't even make out the number that's written here," Franck said.

Mémé brushed the dusting of flour off her forearm. "Twenty-seven million francs."

Franck smiled up at her. "Ah. *Merci.*" It took a few moments for Franck and Mémé to register my stunned silence.

"In old *francs*!" Mémé said, and she and Franck laughed. "New *francs* never did make any sense to me."

"So that means it's listed at 270,000 *francs*." Franck squeezed my knee. "New *francs*." Mémé shrugged her disapproval of this whole new *francs* business and went back to evaluate her dough.

270,000 *francs*. To some that wouldn't seem like much, but we had no income at the moment and now that I was turning my back on the possibility of law as a career, not even a solid prospect of one.

"How much does the price translate into dollars again?"

Franck punched a few numbers into his calculator. "$71,145 Canadian."

Once we were back in Canada, I had no idea what we would do for work. I was quite certain that the salary for a barista at Starbuck's wouldn't pay both a Vancouver rent (astronomical according to my friends who lived there) plus the mortgage on a place in France. Two hundred and seventy thousand. It seemed like a very, very big number – almost as ridiculous as twenty-seven million *francs*.

"Let's go for a walk." Franck grabbed my hand and led me out. "We think better when we're moving." We found ourselves quickly on the path that wound through the vineyards. My legs felt heavy as they moved through the still, sticky air. Thunder rumbled in the distance.

Franck's eyes searched mine. He wanted this house. I knew that he would feel better moving back to Canada knowing that we had a house here that would always be ours. His family frequently told the story of a cousin of Mémé's who'd left for America after the war to be with her soldier love and never returned to France again. Franck didn't want that to be our future.

"We have your grandfather's forty thousand dollars." His thumb rubbed the humid skin in the palm of my hand.

That was true and it *would* help. But if we were to buy the house, did it mean Franck and I were finally embarking on our life as a married couple, or were we just extracting ourselves from the untenable situation in Oxford in order to pitch ourselves into another one?

"I think we should offer the asking price," Franck said, looking down at the pink vineyard dust that swirled around our ankles.

"How are we going to pay the mortgage every month? What if we can't find jobs in Vancouver?" The house needed a lot of work, and as far as renovations – especially in a house several centuries old – neither Franck nor I knew what we were doing. There were so many unknowns.

"It'll work out one way or another," Franck said. "I know that it will."

"But…"

"It *will*." How I wanted to go through life like my husband and be certain that any path I encountered in life would lead somewhere interesting and good. "Remember the fireplace?" Franck's hazel eyes glowed almost gold. "And the cheese cupboard?"

Need seized me by the throat. Nobody could appreciate the cheese cupboard the way I could. I felt just like I did when I was eight and stood contemplating a massive double looping roller coaster in an amusement park in California. Should I get on? The wild part of me itched to jump on the ride and feel the thrill of losing control while the anxious part of me worried a pin was loose and I might plummet to my death.

Franck watched me. He plucked a grape off a vine and popped it in his mouth. "Did you see the date that was carved in the stone at the bottom window of the neighbor's house?"

"*Non.*"

"It said 1789. That must have been when the farm was built. Maître Lefebvre told me it was all one big house that was split up over the centuries."

"1789," I echoed. "The year of the French Revolution." So when the Bastille was being stormed, our house was being built, stone by stone and huge oak beam by huge oak beam. Uh oh. *Our* house? A clap of thunder boomed close by and the clouds began to squeeze out fat drops of rain.

I took a last, fleeting glance at the ground beneath my feet and braced myself for the ride. "OK," I said to Franck. "Let's offer the full amount."

Franck lifted me up and spun me around until the vineyards around us became a green blur. He planted a long kiss on my lips before setting me down – a kiss that made me feel as though I was home already. We grabbed each other's hand and tried to outrun the storm.

We were soaked by the time we got back but we were safely inside before the lightning started to crash all around Franck's house. I hopped in the shower, mainly because I needed a few minutes of solitude to clear my head before we called Le Maître and made it official. I wouldn't go back on what I said – I had been brought up to follow through on my commitments, hence the two years at law school – but I just needed a few minutes of quiet and hot water.

When I emerged from the bathroom, still combing my wet hair, I was confronted with a full-blown celebration in the kitchen. Apparently, Franck had announced to his entire family that we were about to become property owners. Franck's family never really subscribed to that whole "don't count your chickens before they hatch" philosophy that I had been reared on.

"It's not done yet!" I protested to my husband. "We have no idea if they're even going to accept our offer!" I was convinced in the deepest depths of my soul that to boast or even share hopes that something good was in the offing was to jinx that very thing.

"It's never too early to celebrate!" Mémé said and disappeared into the cellar only to reappear a few seconds later brandishing one of the bottles of chilled crémant she always kept on hand for impromptu festivities. "Franck, come here and open this for me!"

A crack of lightning made the windows shake. It was too early. If anything would ruin our chances of pulling this deal off, it would surely be popping the cork on a bottle of crémant.

"Franck," I hissed. "We can't celebrate yet."

Before Franck could answer, Mémé broke into an impromptu rendition of "Le Ban Bourguignon" – a traditional Burgundian drinking song that consisted of turning your hands and signing crescendos of "laa – laa – laaas". It had surely become the Burgundian drinking song over the years precisely because it was hard to screw up even after prodigious wine consumption. Franck rolled his eyes and pulled me towards the door.

"Why not? They're happy because it means we will always be coming back here. Let's just enjoy this moment with them."

"Remember what happened last time," I reminded him. "What if we don't get the house?"

"At least we'll have gotten a celebration out of it."

My heart was skipping beats and I was breathing too fast. "But it could jinx everything!" I had to make him understand.

Franck studied me for a moment. "Instead of having such faith that things will turn out badly, why don't you try to believe that they will turn out just fine - no matter what we do or don't do? Do you really think that whoever is up there in heaven cares if we dance and sing and drink *crémant*?"

"I just think - "

"*Non.*" Franck shook his head. "What you are doing is believing, not thinking. It's a choice. The problem is that you do not believe in something that makes you happy. What's the point of that?"

Mémé came over, linked her arm in Franck's and dragged him to the middle of the kitchen for an impromptu jig. I lingered by the doorway. Could I really just decide to believe something different? A door opened, just like it had when the *Père Bard* had said that in his opinion, God had put us here to have fun. Maybe I should try that.

Still, it was with a vestige of unease — those old habits can feel scary to break — that I smiled at Mémé as she jigged over to me with a full glass in her hand. I tried very hard to let my reservations go.

I had never met anyone who was more gifted for capitalizing on a moment of celebration than Burgundians, and the kitchen was soon full of Ban Bourguignons and one empty bottle of *crémant* quickly became two. Mémé kept leaping up to do impromptu dances of joy around the table. As far as she was concerned it was a done deal. Her cherished Franck was becoming a property owner and even if we were about to embark on that long and evil trip to the hinterlands of Canada, the Magny house — which she already thought of as our house - meant that we would be coming back.

"I just hope I'm not dead before you get the keys!" she laughed. Judging from the way her feet flew over the kitchen floor, I had a pretty strong hunch Mémé would be around for our housewarming.

CHAPTER 11

At some point during the drinking and singing Franck remembered that he still hadn't actually called Le Maître to tell him we were prepared to offer the asking price for the house.

"We need to know the answer by the end of today," I reminded Franck before he went upstairs to phone.

"Right." Franck was a tad wobbly, and grasped on to the doorjamb for support. I hoped he didn't forget because we were leaving in – how were we ever going to pull this off? – three days. Franck came back downstairs after only a few minutes.

"How did he sound?" I asked, but the *crémant* had taken the edge off my former urgency.

"Drunk. But he did say he was going to call the owners right away. Hopefully he remembers."

"What do we do now?"

Franck plucked up his glass and threw his arm around Mémé's shoulder. "We wait by the phone," he chuckled. "We should be getting good at that by now."

After fifteen interminable minutes during which every possible scenario circled in my brain several times over, I pulled Franck's sleeve. "Do you think we should call him back? Maybe he's forgotten," I gasped. "Maybe he's even passed out!"

"I'll wait until eleven o'clock," Franck said. "If we don't hear from him by then, I'll call him." Eleven o'clock in the morning was fifteen minutes away. An eternity.

Eleven o'clock came and went. Franck called again but could only talk to the secretary. Le Maître had gone out for a *rendez-vous*, he was informed, and the secretary had no idea when he would return. We believed her, poor woman.

After lunch Franck pushed back his chair. "Let's go!"

"Where?" I asked. We needed to stay by the phone.

"To his office. We won't leave until we've been able to get him to call the owners."

"You mean you don't even think he's called them?"

Franck threw his linen napkin on the table. "I'm starting to have my doubts."

Fifteen minutes later we had zoomed down through the vineyards to Ladoix-Serrigny. Franck stalked up to the secretary's desk and demanded to see Le Maître.

"*Mais*…I don't know when he'll be in," she protested.

"We'll wait." Franck leaned against the secretary's desk and signalled at me to get comfortable.

The secretary frowned at us. She waved towards the ripped orange plastic chairs and dog-eared *Paris Matches* in the adjacent waiting room. "*Monsieur et Madame Germain*, please take a seat."

Franck's smile didn't veil the steel in his eye. "We'll wait here, *merci*."

The secretary didn't look happy, but she didn't look particularly surprised either. She just shrugged and began typing again as though client protests were something she endured on a regular basis.

There was plenty of time to suck several of the breath mints in a bowl on the secretary's desk and to study the yellowing map of the Côte D'Or's various wine appellations on the wall. I plucked up a copy of the free notary newsletter from a large stack and began to peruse an article about the convoluted French concept of *usufruit* that made my brain go numb. Thank God I wasn't going back to studying law in the fall. But then…what would I be doing? The thought of having no project at all made my hands tremble. What would I be with no project? I wouldn't be a law student, or an entrepreneur, or a promising writer.

I would just be me.

Just then Le Maître breezed in, his tie askew. He granted Franck and me a vague smile that made it clear he didn't recognize us in the slightest, then went on to harangue his secretary about the paperwork concerning the sale of some vines in Morey-Saint-Denis.

"*Bonjour, Maître.*" Franck positioned himself between Le Maître and the door to Le Maître's office, relieving Le Maître of a large pile of the papers that were rapidly slipping from his hold. "Let me help you with that."

"You really shouldn't," Le Maître protested. "Confidential, you know."

"I'll keep my eyes closed," Franck promised. Le Maître found his key and watched with resignation as we marched into his office. Franck set down the papers on Le Maître's cluttered desk and turned to him.

"Have you called the owners of the house with our offer?"

Le Maître squinted at us. "*Quoi?*"

I could feel Franck vibrate with frustration beside me. "The owners of the house we saw together yesterday morning in Magny. I talked to you on the phone a few hours ago and asked you to tell them we would offer the asking price but that our offer only stands for twenty-four hours. You told me you were going to call them right away."

It was clear that Le Maître suffered amnesia about the entire exchange. "*Bah alors…*no time like the present! Shall we call them now?"

"Yes." Franck's teeth were so clenched I was amazed he was able to get the words out. "Let's."

Le Maître picked up his phone and bellowed at his secretary to connect him to the owners of the house in Magny.

Franck and I exchanged a glance. Thank God we had come.

The owners answered after only two rings and Le Maître, after a garrulous *bonjour*, proudly informed them that, after much trouble and toil on his part, he had found a buyer for their house.

"How much?" Le Maître echoed the owner's question. "Let me ask them." He raised an eyebrow at us. "Have you decided how much you'd like to offer?"

With admirable restraint Franck reiterated, "The *asking* price."

Le Maître nodded and conveyed this information to the owners, again giving all credit to himself. A few seconds later he frowned and did a very clumsy job of covering the receiver. "How much *was* the asking price?" he hissed at us.

The secretary slipped into the room just then with a sheet of paper in her hand and cast Franck and me a look of sympathy.

"How much?" Le Maître mouthed at the three of us again.

"Two hundred and seventy thousand francs," we all answered at once. Le Maître plucked his glasses off his desk and waved his secretary away with them. She stood her ground. Whatever she was paid, it wasn't enough.

He cleared his throat. "Of course that's three hundred and twenty thousand francs...*bien sûr*...of course you already know that." He listened for a while without saying anything, then nodded several times. "Right then. I'll tell them."

He hung up the phone, a beatific smile lighting up his face, then picked up a piece of paper on his desk and began studying it with pursed lips. We waited for a few seconds.

The secretary rolled her eyes. "So did they *accept* Monsieur and Madame Germain's offer?"

He glanced up at us again, evidently surprised to still find us there standing in front of his desk. "Of course! Congratulations, by the way."

The secretary crooked her finger at Franck and me. "Follow me. We'll work out all the details."

With light-speed efficiency, the secretary did exactly as she promised. First of all, she phoned the owners back. They were just as bewildered as we had been. She explained everything to them and set up the signing of the *Compromis de Vente* for the next day, only two days before we took the plane to Vancouver. She handed us a stack of photocopied documents.

"The final signing will be three months after that."

"Ah...there's a slight problem," Franck said. "We'll be in Vancouver."

The secretary remained nonplussed. "Do you have any family here?"

"My parents."

"In that case, we'll just set up a power of attorney and have them come in and sign on your behalf."

We had our new project. It was as easy as that.

Two days later we found ourselves signing the *Compromis de Vente* with one of the owners – a tall gentleman who seemed in a hurry to get the signing done and get back for another appointment in Dijon – and the secretary. Le Maître stamped things with his impressive notary seal and congratulated himself repeatedly on his excellent work.

The day we left for Canada, we woke up before the roosters for André to drive to us to Dijon to catch the early train to Paris. As we pulled away from Franck's front gate, Franck asked his father to stop for a moment in front of the church in Magny. André pulled into one of the parking spots across from our house – our house! – stopping under the bright green canopy of the *tilleul* tree.

Franck and I climbed out of the car into the soft morning air of summer and stood on the worn steps of the church, gazing across the street at the little house that would soon be our home in France. Our fingers laced together. The church bell behind us rang five times; the silvery sound didn't rouse the sleepy village. A minute after the last bell had sounded the bell on top of the Mayor's Office began to ring five times.

"The two bells aren't in sync," I observed.

"Anarchist bells." Franck said. "Very French."

Our house would always live by the rhythm of those two bells, one slightly behind the other but both – as far as they were concerned – ringing at the right time.

"*Deux Clochers*," Franck said. Two bell towers. "We should call our house *La Maison des Deux Clochers.*"

When the last ring had finished washing over the tile rooftops I lifted up his hand and planted a kiss on his knuckle. "I like the sound of that."

CHAPTER 12

When we had left Burgundy for Vancouver four months earlier, the hollyhocks had been in full bloom and the vineyards were a riot of green. Now André's car splashed through puddles the size of small lakes on the way up to Villers-la-Faye after picking Franck and me up at the Beaune train station. The few vineyard workers who were pruning the vines were hunched over in vast black rubber capes, looking wet and miserable in the sheeting rain.

December in Burgundy, I remembered now, was a different *paire de manches,* or pair of sleeves, from July.

We had already planned to spend several hours looking through our newly purchased house the next day, but now all we wanted was a bed. Dusk was falling and we had been travelling for more than thirty hours.

As our representative, André had signed the Act of Sale last month and we had paid our first mortgage payment only two weeks ago. It was ours - this little stone house built in the year of the Revolution would come into view in just a few seconds, as soon as we rounded the corner.

Franck leaned over me, squinting out of the rain-splattered window and asked me if I still didn't believe in praying to the Virgin Mary. I wondered if he could feel the erratic rhythm of my heart skipping in my chest. I was pretty certain I knew what he was thinking...we had a little over four months to do all of the renovations, and a budget of fifteen thousand dollars.

Oh yes, and this unedifying state of affairs was mostly my fault.

Entirely my fault, truth be told.

Back in Vancouver I had gone through the motions of researching how to convert my British law degree into a Canadian law degree.

"It's complicated," I told people when they asked when I would start practising. "It takes time."

I had phoned the law society and filled out all the forms for them to review my situation, as well as talked to several high school friends of mine who were practising lawyers. But the motions were just that – motions. They were hollow inside, not fleshed out with any passion or desire. All my ambition had scurried off somewhere.

It wasn't the conversion of my law degree that invaded my daydreams during the four months in Vancouver. It was the cheese cupboard in our *petite maison* and that ancient door in the kitchen and the wide stone stairs and the crooked walls. These would be my responsibility now. I not only cherished such stewardship, I took it very seriously. Yet somehow in my mind's eye, I always pictured our house looking exactly on our return as it had for our departure in July: blooming, stunning, blue-skied, full of hope. . .not to mention being a cinch to renovate in four months.

One night, a few weeks after Franck and I had moved into our snug Vancouver apartment, we were lying in bed listening to the sirens wailing down West Broadway and debating how we would pay our monthly French mortgage payment. I was nestled in that spot between Franck's shoulder and his neck that seemed made just for me. Given that our monthly income was currently only about twenty five hundred dollars and that we had to pay exorbitant rent on our tiny Vancouver apartment, the mortgage amount was huge to us, almost unmanageable.

We lay intertwined in the dark. My thoughts drifted from our mortgage payment to the beaten iron latches on our cheese cupboard. Maybe when we had renovated the house, some of our friends could come and stay. Maybe some of them would find the latches on the kitchen door and the ornately wrought metal banister on the stairs as entrancing as I did. It would be amazing to set up the house so that Franck and I could welcome a lot of people and share the experience of living in an authentic French village for a few days or a few weeks.

Then it hit me. Why didn't we try to rent out the house when we weren't using it? At best, we would be able to use the house for about a month every year. It seemed a travesty to have the house all shut up and empty in the interim.

"Wouldn't it be great if we could share our house with anyone who was interested?" I whispered in the dark to Franck. "We could charge a bit of rent – enough to cover the mortgage. And even if we couldn't quite manage to do that, any little bit would help, *n'est-ce pas?*"

Franck lay beside me, silent for a long while.

"Who on earth would want to come to vacation in Burgundy?" Franck said at last.

"Franck," I reminded him, "my mom and dad have taken two *very* expensive bike trips to Burgundy in the last five years. And they loved Beaune and they loved the wine and they loved the food. They just loved the *Frenchness* of it all."

Franck made a disbelieving sound in the back of his throat. "Magny-les-Villers is not exactly Paris."

How could I make him see? To Franck, Burgundy was just his *home* – simple and familiar like the Pacific Northwest was for me.

"Do you remember your first ferry ride from Vancouver to Victoria that very first Christmas after you had moved to Montreal?"

Franck nodded.

Growing up on Vancouver Island, I had been brought up resenting the ferry trip between our island and the mainland. Like most fellow islanders, to me British Columbia's ferries meant reheated Baron O' Beef, unintelligible safety announcements over the PA, and cancelled sailings. I would invariably spend the crossing hunkered down in the cafeteria with a stale coffee in a Styrofoam cup and a trashy magazine. That was where I headed on Franck's first ferry trip, but he grabbed my arm and dragged me out onto the deck into the freezing December air.

"This is amazing!" he shouted over the noise of the engines, his head whipping to and fro to scan the scenery. We hadn't even left the ferry terminal. He installed us on top of one of the wooden life vest lockers on the deck and we stayed there for the whole journey, huddling together against the cold. He couldn't stop exclaiming over the beauty and the grandeur of our route through the Gulf Islands.

That trip opened my eyes to what had been in front of me my whole life: secret coves, cedar fringed cliffs, and even a pod of orca whales that swam alongside the ship for a few minutes. I needed to do the same for him with Burgundy.

"That's what's so great about this idea." I wound my leg around his and ran my finger lazily up and down his bicep. "I know what North Americans would want out of a vacation rental in France."

"A nearby McDonalds?"

I gave Franck a pinch. "No, not fast food - a comfortable mattress, a proper shower, functioning toilets, but lots of history and period details too." He traced little swirls on the nape of my neck, thoughtful. "And you, *mon chéri*, have the local connections that can make everything happen," I added.

Whenever we talked about our jobs in Vancouver we became stressed and distant but I had noticed Burgundy had a magical way of binding us back together again.

The swirls became light kisses. "Maybe it could work," he admitted.

Shortly after that Franck fell asleep. I lay staring at the path of headlights criss-crossing our ceiling. We could furnish the house with all of those amazing old *armoires* and tables found so readily in the *brocantes* all over Burgundy. I would make sure the bathroom was brand new and that we installed a proper wall hook-up for the shower. I would also find out as much about the history of the house as I could so that I could leave its story for our guests to read. Maybe other people would be as enthralled as me to think that the house was built in the same year as the Revolution, and that those stone steps had been quarried by men who were concerned not only about their stone cutting, but also about the fact that in Paris the aristocrats were having their heads lopped off.

"But who are we going to rent it *to*?" Franck asked me the next morning over breakfast. "How can we let people know that we are doing this?"

This gave me pause. As certain as I was that there were kindred spirits who would want to stay at our little French house, I hadn't given any thought yet as to how we would actually find them.

"We'll start by sending a letter to the people who came to our wedding last summer, and ask them to spread the word." I said the words as soon as they popped into my head.

"That's actually a very good idea."

"*Merci.*" I bowed.

As Franck finished eating I slipped off to my computer. I opened an empty Word document and began typing. I had to put in a date when people could start renting it, I realized as I got about half way down. I did a quick calculation in my head. We'd been planning to go over at Christmas, but we couldn't leave our jobs here for too long. Since we had been back in Vancouver, I had been working for the family company trying to sell earplugs to the managers of a chain of optical stores. They were called "earbugs" and were a hard sell from the name on downwards.

What needed to be done? Taking down the wallpaper – that couldn't be too hard - repainting the heck out of the place, redoing the bathroom and a bit of the kitchen, repainting the shutters. All that wouldn't take very long at all. Four months, tops. That would give us all the time we needed and then some. Besides, I had to be back in Oxford on May 1 for my graduation ceremony. I typed down in the letter that our house would be available for rent as of Mayday.

Once I'd finished my letter, I found the email list for the hundred or so people who attended our wedding reception in Victoria, attached it, and hit "send." Two days later Franck cobbled together a rudimentary website.

Three days later I had a call from the brother and sister-in-law of one of my Mom's friends who had been at our wedding. They wanted to rent our house for the first two weeks in May. I dragged a rather stunned looking Franck down the road to Solly's Bagelry to eat a celebratory breakfast.

I leaned back heavily in the seat as the car pulled in front of the wooden gate to *chez Germain*. Things didn't appear quite in the same light back here in Burgundy as they did in Vancouver. We had exactly four months and ten days to get our house ready for our first renters, and the five groups of renters that followed immediately after them. My plan had worked even better than I could have imagined. Only the wooden statue of the Virgin knew if this was good or bad.

The next morning over a late breakfast (we had slept a solid fourteen hours due to jetlag, not to mention a certain reluctance to face reality) Franck's parents presented Franck with the huge clutch of keys that I had first seen in Le Maître's hand four months earlier. Franck passed them ceremoniously over to me. They were substantial in my hands and had a metallic whiff of permanence. There were at least fifteen keys of different shapes and sizes on the interlocking rings.

André sighed. "It's all yours now." He clearly relished the thought that our house was no longer his responsibility. Given the gushing drainpipe we had seen last night as we drove past, I could hardly blame him.

Mémé marched into the kitchen from the dining room, bringing the smells of butter and flour with her. She was staying at *chez Germain* over Christmas and she had already informed us that her plan for the day was to stuff several hundred escargots.

"Are you finished with breakfast yet?" she asked us, dropping a kiss on her beloved Franck's head. "I have a lot of cooking to do." I found that hard to believe as almost every surface of the kitchen was covered in freshly baked bread, mini-quiches, mini-pizzas, and two *gâteaux de savoie* that she had informed us were for her *Bûches de Noël*.

"More cooking?" Michèle asked. "What else can you possibly need to cook? Besides, we're almost out of flour."

"I noticed that." Mémé handed over a neatly penned list to André. "I will need you to go into Beaune and get these things for me. Don't try to palm any of those generic products off on me. I can only work with *mes produits*." André stared down at the list and his mouth tightened. Mémé whipped her dishtowel over her shoulder. "I'll be needing those ingredients soon," she said, nodding towards the door.

Michèle took a deep breath and rolled her eyes at Franck and me.

"Let's go have a shower." Franck pulled me up. When Franck had shut the bathroom door behind us he said, "I think now is a good time to go and inspect our house if we don't want to be drafted in as sous-chefs.

Once we were clean, we let ourselves out the door and scurried across the frosty courtyard to the stone barn where we found André. He had wisely embarked on a thorough cleaning project of the barn to keep himself out of the way. Franck asked if we could borrow the Citroën and André took the keys from his pocket, handing them over to us. He waved good-bye as he shut the courtyard gate behind us and I'm sure he hightailed it back into the tranquility of the barn.

I cranked up the heat. "Maybe we should move to our place sooner rather than later."

Franck looked grim. "We're also going to need to buy a car, you know. My dad needs this one to get back and forth to work. "

Merde. I had never considered the obvious need for a car, nor had I budgeted for it. I put my hands in front of the air vent, but the air coming out was frigid.

"Do you realize how cold it is going to be in our house?" Franck asked me. "*Chez nous?*"

"I think I'm about to find out."

Franck slid the car into one of the two parking spots in front of the church in Magny. There was a nervous flutter in my chest. It felt similar to the one I had when my friend Sandrine and I were driving to Franck's house to pick up him and Stéphanie the night after Franck and I had first met. Within an hour of being introduced we were making out on the dance floor of a local discothèque. I knew I liked Franck, but I figured he probably only wanted a one-night fling like most other guys. Then, as now, I was filled with equal parts excitement and uncertainty.

I glanced up at the *tilleuls* which arched over our car. In the summer they had been covered with an explosion of pale green leaves. Now the leaves had fallen and the branches were all cut off, leaving only truncated stumps like a passel of fists gesticulating at the sky.

I clutched the bunch of keys as we crunched across the pea gravel that only scantly covered the frozen dirt of the passageway underneath our house. The stone stairs were frosty. I held on to the gray metal railing so as not to slip. Was I still going to see potential in this place? I rubbed the keys for luck.

Franck creaked open the metal door of the veranda. His parents had told us they had gone and unlocked it the day before.

"You do the honors," he said, waving at the wad of keys in my hand.

I looked down and realized I had no idea which key opened the front door. "This could take a while." I slid the biggest, most ancient looking key into the wooden door. I tried to turn it but it didn't catch. I tried several others while Franck began to jump up and down on the spot to warm up.

Finally I wiggled in a mangled key – one of the last ones on the ring

I hadn't tried - but it didn't seem to work either. Frustrated, I gave the door a shove with my shoulder. It swung open. The arctic air inside, combined with the overpowering stench of mothballs, stole my breath.

"How can the inside of a house be colder than outside?"

"I told you," Franck said.

"But how?"

Franck tapped the wall behind us. "Welcome to the joys of very old houses. The stone traps in the cold and the humidity." He pulled me toward him and planted a kiss on the numb tip of my nose. He had given me many lectures on the downsides of older houses through the fall, but I hadn't really listened. "You never really believed me until now, did you?"

I shivered. "I guess not. *Mes excuses.*" A thought struck me. "I never really paid attention to what kind of heating system they had in here." Please let it be central heating. The question hadn't so much as flitted through my head in July.

"Luckily I did," Franck said.

He flicked on the single light bulb in the living room and led me over to a behemoth beige metallic unit sitting against the far wall of the living room, underneath my beloved cheese cupboard. "I asked Le Maître about it while you were admiring the hinges on the kitchen door. He said these units are some kind of old brick refractor system. We'll have to replace them with radiators of course, but at least they'll heat things up for the time being. "

Franck leaned down to try to coax the unit into turning on while I drifted off to inspect the rest of our house. Franck's parents had warned us that it was still packed with furniture, and that the sellers had asked at the signing for us to call them when we arrived to set up a time for them to come and move it all away. They weren't kidding. There seemed to be even more furniture in the tiny house than there had been in July. Or maybe that was just an impression, as the brick heaters took up so much floor space.

I ran a finger over the massive wooden buffet in the living room that actually touched the more than nine foot high wallpapered ceiling. The wood was so dark that it was almost black. The bottom doors were embellished with carved dragons and scary looking birds.

"I can't wait to get rid of this," I said to Franck. Before he answered the stench of burning rubber filled the air. "Is it supposed to smell like that?" I began to cough.

I hurried over to the window, wrenched it open and flung open the shutters, just like Papa in "The Night Before Christmas". The shutters in that story must have been sturdier than ours. There was the ominous sound of splintering wood, then one of our shutters crashed to the street below.

"*Merde*," I murmured. Definitely not a good omen.

Franck joined me at the window and looked dispassionately down at what remained of the shutter. "Unfortunately, you'll have to go and get that by yourself," he said. "I can't leave the heater right now or I'm afraid I might end up burning the whole house down."

When I came back up and put the pieces of wood on the table, the burning smell had become even more acrid. "Is that normal?"

"I'll guess we'll know in a few minutes if we don't pass out or die from carbon monoxide poisoning first," Franck said. He stood up and gave the radiator a kick. I sidled closer to the window and the fresh air.

Franck, meanwhile, crossed the room and studied the hideous buffet himself. "I'm not sure I agree with you," he said. "It's hard to tell with the wallpaper and everything, but I think I actually kind of like this thing."

I stared at my husband, feeling like I had never really known him up until this moment. Had he really become such a stranger to me in the past two years? I put a hand on the windowsill to steady myself. Our time in Vancouver had been so busy with finding an apartment and then work. We never really had time to reconnect and rebuild after Oxford. We had a big chasm to bridge, and something told me that these next four months would be crucial to our future together.

Franck patted the sad looking plaid tweed couch that was pushed up against the wall beside the buffet. "And this will be the conjugal bed." He gave me a wink that turned into a gasping cough at the puff of dust that billowed up. As far as beds went, it didn't exactly invite languorous reconciliations.

I reminded myself that every journey starts with a first step. I sidled over and sat down gingerly on the couch. The springs poked the backs of my thighs through my jeans. My eyes began to water. I sneezed six times in a row.

From this angle, the buffet looked as though it had every intention of squashing me in my sleep. The open window let in the cold winter air, but it was no match for the stench of burning rubber coming from the strange radiator. This wasn't how I had pictured our first visit back to our house at all. I had pictured something far more...well...romantic and comfortable. This was an adventure, I reminded myself sternly, and adventures were rarely comfortable.

"Home Sweet Home," I said to Franck. I reached up and pulled him down beside me. As for the romance, that was up to us.

CHAPTER 13

Both of us started to feel wonky with jetlag, and possibly radiator fumes. We needed to eat and take the car back so we headed back to *chez Germain* for lunch.

"When should we plan to move in?" I wondered out loud, as Franck pulled out of the parking spot in front of the church. A week, or better yet two, from now sounded about right.

"After lunch," Franck said. "We'll sleep at our house tonight."

I thought back to the thick cloud of dust that had billowed up from the couch. "Tonight? On that couch?"

"*Bien sûr.*"

"I'll die of an allergy attack...or of that *armoire* falling over on me during the night."

"Laura, it's not going to get any more comfortable. We only have four months. We have to start right away." Franck was preoccupied during lunch and told us as we were finishing up the cheese course that he had already arranged with his friend Olivier to have our cafés at his house. I knew that was a lie, but I wasn't going to argue.

Olivier was one of Franck's oldest friends; he lived across the street from Franck's parents and just up from the village *boulangerie* with his wife Dominique and their son Marcel.

"Don't get me wrong. I love Olivier," I said to Franck as we bundled up in our coats. "But don't we have other things we should be doing this afternoon, like finding a clean set of sheets for the sofa bed?"

"First we need to consult with the *L'Oracle*."

"The Oracle?"

"Yes. Olivier is like the village oracle. You saw how much work that house needs. Olivier will give us good advice. *Wise* advice," Franck added, tapping his temple.

Luckily *L'Oracle* was in. We were kissed on both cheeks and quickly seated at the kitchen table where Olivier was enjoying an after lunch cigarette. Dominique poured us thick and bitter cups of espresso. Marcel pulled at our legs from under the table and pleaded for *sucre*.

"He's obsessed with sugar cubes," Dominique explained. "Don't give him any." I saw Olivier's hand slip under the table with a few cubes in his palm.

Olivier then turned to Franck. "You've got that troubled look."

Franck didn't need any further encouragement. He plunged into a detailed explanation of our house dilemma: the mammoth amount of renovations needed, the fact that we had no idea where to start and no contacts in the trades, our woefully limited budget...it took several minutes, during which the room started to tilt and my heart began to beat erratically. I sucked in as much air as I could, but it didn't seem like enough. What did I think I was doing, embarking on this crazy venture?

I twisted my hands in my lap and tried to concentrate on Olivier. He soaked in every word that came out of Franck's mouth. Even though he was shorter than me, and looked ten years younger than both Franck and I, Olivier had the definite air of a wise man around him. Even in *École primaire*, Franck had told me, people sought him out for level-headed advice and a sympathetic, yet never complacent, ear.

I had done exactly that two years before, the day before my wedding. I had been decorating the wine cellar in Nuits-Saint-Georges for the reception, trying to mediate between two of Franck's garrulous extended family members about the correct way to position the crêpe paper flowers between the stones in the walls. The squabbling continued despite my best attempts at diplomacy and I eventually stormed up the stairs for a much-needed breath of fresh air. Exiting the cellar, I stood up too fast and whacked my head on the vaulted stone entrance so hard that I saw not only stars, but planets too. I swore viciously, clutched my head, and sank down beside Olivier, who was perched on the little wall at the top of the stairs, enjoying a cigarette, *comme d'habitude.*

"*Ça va* Laura?" he asked. To most people I would have answered a stony and completely untrue "*ça va*" but something about the tone of his voice – like he actually cared – or the crinkles at the corners of his eyes, gave me pause.

"This wedding business is more trouble than it's worth," I grumbled. "I'm exhausted. All day long people have been accosting me with questions like 'when do the dishes arrive tomorrow at the cellar?', 'when are you supposed to pick up the croquembouche?', 'do you want the *soupe à l'oignon* with or without emmenthal on top?' Every question makes me realize how much could go wrong tomorrow."

Olivier clicked his tongue.

"My father just informed me that he checked the weather forecast and that it's going to rain." I plucked the cigarette out of Olivier' fingers and took a deep drag, asthma be damned. "Franck and I should have eloped to Las Vegas."

Olivier patted me on the knee. "Tomorrow will be the best day of your life, Laura."

I snorted. "Yes. That is if the croquembouche magically shows up and we find someone who can pick up the flowers from Beaune and - "

"Tomorrow will be the best of your life," he interrupted. "None of those other things matter. What matters is that tomorrow you are marrying Franck and you will be surrounded by people who love both of you. Everything else will work itself out. Even if it doesn't, it won't matter. That's how it was for me. That's how it will be for you. *Promis.*"

I opened my mouth and then shut it again. I passed his cigarette back, then leaned over and gave his scratchy unshaven cheek a kiss.

"*Merci*, Olivier."

It did rain the next day but Olivier had been right – it didn't matter. Besides, as Franck reminded me as we led the wedding party in the traditional walk from his house to the village mayor's office, *mariage pluvieux, mariage heureux* or "a rainy marriage is a happy marriage". The croquembouche had even showed up right on time, although I'm still not sure by what miraculous means.

"Leave it with me," Olivier said when Franck reached the end of our tale of renovation woes. "I need to think about your dilemma for a day or two." My heart felt soothed, like it had done after I had talked to the Virgin Mary statue in the church in Magny.

Then Franck launched into "Franck and Laura's problems - Part Two: A Car."

Olivier, contrary to Franck and me, had always been interested in cars. Franck had very much the same view on vehicles as me, meaning that as long as they had four wheels and moved in a forward direction one was as good as any other. Franck and I needed a used car – a very, *very* inexpensive used car. And we were poorly equipped to come head to head with unscrupulous used car dealers.

"*La!*" Olivier exclaimed. "There I can help you right away. I'm going to send you to René."

"I thought he had moved down to Provence after his divorce," Franck said. I was intrigued. I had heard a lot about this enigmatic René from Franck and his friends. His first claim to fame was that he talked so continuously that his friends couldn't figure out exactly how he breathed. The second was that he and his now ex-wife decided to get divorced at their very own wedding reception, mere minutes after making the first slice in their wedding cake.

"He's moved back to Louhans. He works in a garage there. He didn't find people very friendly in the south."

"Maybe they weren't deaf enough," Franck said.

Olivier smiled. "If they weren't when he arrived, they surely are now."

It was settled. Olivier would call René that very moment and see if he wouldn't take us under his wing to find a used and cheap car.

When he hung up the phone, Olivier took a long, evaluating look at my husband. "Now, I need you to do a favour for me."

"Name it," said Franck.

He walked over to the huge ornamental buffet against the far wall that had been his grandmother's and which looked like the long-lost twin of ours. He extracted an unlabeled dark green glass bottle from its murky depths as well as a well-worn pack of Tarot playing cards.

"Taste some of this *calvados* and tell me what you think, and play a hand of tarot with Dominique and me." Franck's face relaxed instantly; I didn't have the heart to remind him that we still had a million things to do. They could wait, I supposed, one more day.

After our visit with Olivier, we returned to our rubber smelling money pit with not only lighter heads, but lighter hearts. We tossed the cushions off the sofa, trying to ignore the dust that billowed off with them, and pulled out the rusty pull-out bed.

"Our first night in our new house," Franck raised a suggestive brow.

I sneezed.

We fit on the sheets we had brought from Franck's house and plopped down fresh pillows. I must have been exhausted because our bed looked almost inviting. I turned my back on the looming buffet and stripped off my clothes. I wasn't going to look at it tonight, or even think of it falling on me.

"I'm going to have a quick bath to warm up," Franck said. He plopped down a huge wad of mail and brochures on top of our duvet. "I found this in our mailbox. Do you want to start sorting through it? It's probably mostly ads."

I snuggled, shivering, under the duvet. "Hurry back," I said.

With my head pleasantly buzzing and the feel of clean sheets as a barrier between me and the rotting sofa bed, I flipped through the brochures and ads until I came across a thick beige envelope with Le Maître's dark blue seal stamped on the upper corner.

I pulled out the wad of official looking papers entitled "*Acte de Vente*" – the final Act of Sale that proved this house was really and truly ours. I'd had too much *kir* to do more than flip through the pages of French legalese. I paused when I reached the house plan and stared hard at it, hoping for a flash of inspiration as to the best strategy to attack our renovations.

The house looked much smaller on paper. I narrowed my eyes at the piece of paper in front of me. A lot of alterations and mutations had surely happened since 1789. Maybe it was an old house plan. My eyes flicked to the stamp from the land registry at the bottom of the page. It was dated from two months ago.

All of the *kir* in my system evaporated instantaneously. It wasn't just that the house looked small on the plan. It was missing some essential rooms, such as the one I was lying in at that moment.

"Franck!" I hollered.

I flipped back and forth through the *Acte de Vente*, paying close attention now. There had to be a rectified version of the house plan as we bought it: two bedrooms, a tiny kitchen, the hallway, the living room, the bathroom, and the WC...except that there wasn't. There was only that one plan and it showed that our entire house, the one we had paid two hundred and seventy thousand francs for, consisted of only our two bedrooms. No kitchen. No living room. No bathroom or WC. Where were they? That was when I noticed the thick red line that halved them off and counted the missing rooms as part of our next-door neighbour's house.

Et merde.

"*Quoi*?" Franck came running back into the living room, drying his hair with an old towel.

"We didn't buy the whole house." I waved the sheaf of papers at him. "We only bought two rooms of it!"

"What are you talking about?" He climbed into bed beside me and pulled me towards him. "Come here." I hit him over the head with the *Acte de Vente*.

"Listen to me! According to this, for two hundred and seventy thousand francs, we only bought the two bedrooms."

Franck sat up and snatched the document from my hands. His eyes darted back and forth across the plan like minnows.

"*Merde*," he said, rolling his "r" as only a true Burgundian can do.

"What are we going to do?"

Franck glanced at the tiny alarm clock we'd set up beside our bed. "There's nothing we can do now. I'll call Le Maître in the morning." He studied the documents again and sighed deeply.

"This is crazy," I said. "This can't be happening."

Franck sighed deeply. "You're wrong there. It can be happening. Crazy things happen in France all the time."

I woke up feeling more exhausted than when I had gone to bed.

The tightness of Franck's features told me that his dreams hadn't exactly been peaceful either. Before he even kissed me *"bonjour"* he warned me, "Don't try to talk to the neighbour. Let me take care of it. It has to be man to man."

Monsieur De Luca was the neighbour in question and, according to the land registry of the Côte D'Or, also owner of two thirds of our house. He wasn't from either Magny-les-Villers or Villers-la-Faye which, as far as everyone from the villages was concerned, meant he was an outsider. For reasons that remained murky to us, Monsieur De Luca had managed to mortally offend all three of the *grand-mères* who shared our common courtyard. We had heard vague mutterings that he was "land-crazy" and hell bent on buying up every last piece of pea gravel in our cluster of homes. The father and his son, who also lived with him, were from burly Mediterranean stock and were rumored to enjoy frequent brawls, often with each other.

All of those cases that I had poured over in the law library during my two years at Oxford sprung to life. They had taught me that when it came right down to it most people were cynical and greedy. I was certain that Monsieur De Luca would not be willing to give us back our rooms for free.

"I don't like the idea of you going to talk to him alone," I said to Franck as we folded away our bed.

"That's the way it has to be," Franck said, grim. "Maybe I won't have to though. I'll call Le Maître first and the land registry if need be. I may be able to fix things that way."

There was nothing for me to do except have my shower. I shivered in the unheated bathroom. Of all the problems I had imagined when we bought this house I never could have come up with this, not in my wildest imaginings. My teeth clacked together as I stripped off my many layers of jogging pants and sweatshirts and I climbed into our turquoise iron tub. I quickly discovered that our hot water tank held just about enough hot water for a minute and a half of showering before it turned ice cold. I hated this bath. I hated the teeny water tank. Even more I hated the fact that it was our neighbor who owned them both.

An uncomfortable suspicion began to creep up my spine – maybe my *"non"* to Mr. Partridge had been, like he believed, a momentary lapse of sanity due to the stress of Finals. What if this whole French house project was a huge mistake?

By the time I stalked back into the living room my shock had morphed into anger. Judging from the sound of Franck's voice as he talked on the phone in those strident tones that one Frenchman uses to talk over what another Frenchman is saying, I wasn't the only one.

"But there's been a terrible error!" he kept repeating, until his sheer pugnacity seemed to get through to the person on the other end of the line. He nodded his head, said "*d'accord*" a few times and then scrawled something down on a piece of paper he balanced on his knee. He hung up.

"I suppose there's no hot water left."

I decided to take that as a hypothetical question. "Who was that?"

"*Le Cadastre.*"

"Who's *Le Cadastre?*"

He held up the house plan. "The land registrar. He is the only guy who can correct this mess."

Hope rose in my chest.

"Don't be too overjoyed. He can't come until next week. The whole office is closing up shop for Christmas."

The hope plummeted.

"What about *Le Maître*? Did you call him?" I demanded.

"Yes, while you were using up all the hot water " We were both angry and unfortunately the only people available to yell at were each other.

"And?"

"He told me to call the *cadastre*."

"Did he even apologize, or offer to have us go in and look over the documents with him, or anything?"

Franck rolled his eyes. "Of course not."

"Son-of-a-"

"A French notary cannot admit he has made a mistake, just like a French doctor. He blamed the *cadastre* and I knew it wasn't worth wasting my time arguing the point. I suspected the *cadastre* would be the one who could sort this out anyway."

I let out a howl of frustration. We had to wait a whole week with this hanging over our heads?

"Just think…" Franck got off the couch and patted me on the shoulder. "If you had chosen law you would be dealing with this type of thing every day."

I snorted. Of course, the actual work – dealing with conflicts day in and day out – would have been a nightmare. Still, the security of actually *having* a respectable job sounded very seductive right about now.

I wrenched open the window and threw open the disintegrating white shutters. The stumps of the *tilleuls* in front of the church across the street were white with frost. Black spots danced in front of my eyes. I couldn't seem to get enough of the icy morning air in my lungs no matter how deeply I breathed. The world felt unbalanced and full of hidden dangers.

I blinked and caught sight of Madame Parigot, the mother of Franck's winemaker friend Amélie whose family *domaine* was just up the road, as she trundled down the road towards the church. I watched her, hoping a distraction would ward off the tsunami of panic that was bearing down on me. She took a hefty key from her pocket and unlocked the door to the church. She happened to look up in my direction and waved at me, a sturdy presence with her steel gray bun and sensible winter coat. I waved back, trying to appear sane. With a smile, she disappeared inside.

Franck had told me before that Madame Parigot was the caretaker of the village church: changing faded flowers for fresh ones, sweeping the floor, and making sure none of the village children messed with the wooden statue of the Virgin Mary. She was known throughout the village as an extremely religious woman. I could picture her inside the church, moving respectfully in the stained glass silence. How I wanted some of that peace.

Maybe I just hadn't persisted long enough with law. Had I given up just short of the golden ring? Worse still, had I dragged Franck into this mistake with me? I hadn't quite finished whipping myself with this thought when Franck came back in the room, dressed and drying off his spiky black hair with a towel.

"Now that *mes testicules* are frozen off," he said, an accusing look in his dark eye, "I'm going to go over and try to talk to the neighbor."

"I'll come." Anything would be better than standing here waiting to hear that the neighbour wanted us to pay an extortionate amount for something we had already bought.

"*Non.*" Franck was firm. "You have to trust me on this."

"What am I supposed to do then?" I demanded, terrified at the idea of being left alone with my own thoughts.

Franck crooked a finger and I followed him into the kitchen where we had stockpiled a bunch of old tools his dad had lent us. He passed me a rusted scraper and a desiccated sponge.

"You can start scraping off the wallpaper. "

I started in the far bedroom. At least that room was undisputedly ours. Damned if I was going to get on my knees and strip somebody else's wallpaper.

Here the brown and orange flowers that spangled the walls of the living room had given way to a flurry of blues and greens. I filled a chipped ceramic bowl full of freezing water from the kitchen sink, squirted in some rosemary-mint dish soap, dipped the sponge in and started soaking a patch of wallpaper. I hadn't even lifted the scraper before a wet patch of wallpaper peeled back and slithered down to the floor beside me. Underneath it there was another layer of wallpaper – this a far older looking pattern of periwinkle blue stripes and orange roses. I soaked it but it wasn't nearly as obliging. I scraped away on the same little five inch by five inch patch, searching for the bare wall like a miner searching for diamonds. I hadn't thought I would enjoy this at all but it was strangely preoccupying, not to mention the fact that it distracted me from listening too hard for the sounds of a brawl from next door.

The older paper with the stripes and roses must have been stuck on with some sort of super glue made from horse hooves or pig ears way back when. I began to sweat despite the fact that the bedroom had no radiator and the temperature was probably hovering near zero. Millimeter by millimeter, I scraped. Finally I began to make out something behind it that didn't look like wallpaper. I picked up the pace, my scraper rasping back and forth over the uneven surface. Maybe there would be a fresco under here depicting the seasons of the vineyards! That wasn't unheard of in old houses. A band of deep blue revealed itself. And then lower down another band of bottle green. Not a fresco then. I sat back on my heels to look at it from a bit further away. It looked instead as though the wall had been painted to *look* like wallpaper. I attacked the mystery again with even more vigour until a particularly energetic scrape dislodged a chunk of plaster from the wall. *Merde.*

There was no way I could hide it. When Franck came back it would be the first thing he would see.

I cocked an ear, but there was only silence. That could either be a very good or a very bad sign. I started to wonder if maybe Monsieur de Luca had killed Franck and was busy hiding his body in the old well in their courtyard, then I forced myself to look back at the hole in the wall. At least it was a manageable problem.

I stuck my finger in it and my fingertips met cold rock. I must have dug down to the original stone structure of the walls. The hair on the back of my neck prickled. Someone had piled these rocks around at the same time as the beheading of Marie Antoinette in Paris. I knelt down to collect the bits of plaster and debris that had fallen on the floor. They scratched my hand and I looked at them more closely. The mortar contained little pieces of crushed glass and stone as well as bits of horsehair. *Revolutionary* horsehair! Incredible, yet somehow I didn't think Franck would be transported as I was by the historical significance of the hole.

Another few chunks of plaster tumbled down like a mini-avalanche while I was still inspecting my treasures. Just then I heard Franck's footsteps on the veranda.

"Where are you Laura?" he called out.

"Bedroom," I answered quietly, wondering how I could cover up my achievement.

He strode around the corner and his eyes went from me to the hole and then back to me again.

"*Et merde. Et merde, et merde, et MERDE!*" I couldn't figure out if he meant the hole or Monsieur de Luca. Perhaps both.

"How did it go?" I stood up and tried to dust the plaster bits off my thighs. "What did he say?"

Franck leaned over the top of me and touched the side of the hole. More plaster crumbled away under his fingertips. "I was praying the walls wouldn't be in this state."

"Look!" I held out my hand. "I think this may be Revolutionary-era horsehair! I found it in the plaster. Can you believe it?"

Franck gifted me with an icy stare and kicked the wall, unleashing an impressive shower of plaster. "The humidity has gotten into them." He said 'humidity' with the same tone one would use to say 'gangrene' to a soldier in the trenches.

"I'm sure we can fix them. What did Monsieur de Luca say?"

Franck ignored my question. "Does my wife have a special skill in plastering that she has been hiding from me until now?"

My eyes shifted back to the hole. "Not exactly." I was, on the other hand, convinced that Franck could develop plastering skills in no time. I also sensed, however, that this wasn't the most auspicious moment to declare my faith in him.

"With these old walls everything can fall around our ears, and until the wallpaper is off and you start going at it, you just don't know." He scanned the walls around us, worry growing in his eyes. "This could be a much bigger job than we bargained for. I'm not sure we will be able to get it done by May."

"We have to get it done by May." We had accepted - and spent - the deposits our prospective guests had sent to us. They had booked their plane tickets and their rental cars. We couldn't cancel on them.

Franck's index finger twitched on his right hand. He was dying for a cigarette.

"We only have to worry about these two rooms until the plans are sorted out," I said. "What did Monsieur de Luca say?"

Franck turned and stalked into the kitchen, his finger still twitching. I followed and watched him, concerned, as he slumped down on one of the mismatched wooden chairs. "He agrees that none of this house is his…"

"That's *perfect*!" I made a move to hug Franck but he stopped me with a quick hand gesture. "However, he wants to talk to his notary about it."

Two years in law school had been long enough to learn that consulting one's legal team was rarely a precursor to a simple resolution. I sat down in the other wooden chair.

"Let's summarize." If I wasn't logical, I would be swept away with another wave of fear. "We have bought a third of a house for the price of a full one and even that third is looking like it might fall down around us. We may be engaging in an expensive legal battle, and we have tons of work to do on this house before the first of May with no idea how to do it or where to start. Is that about it?"

"We don't have much money," Franck added.

"Oh yes. I forgot about that."

"We don't have a car."

"I forgot about that too."

Franck rapped his knuckles on the scarred wooden kitchen table. "And in about a week or so, the seller's children will be coming to collect all the furniture, so we won't have anywhere to sit, eat, sleep, or *faire l'amour.*"

I didn't think my heart could sink any lower, but it did. "And we have no money to buy new stuff," I confirmed.

"Correct."

"Christmas is in four days and we haven't bought anyone presents yet."

"Right." Franck nodded.

I dropped my head to the table and began to laugh. It was so ridiculous, what else could we do? I heard Franck begin to chuckle above me.

"So, what the hell do we do?" I asked without lifting my head up.

"We give up," Franck said.

"We can't give up!" My head snapped up. There were our future guests, of course, but I couldn't live with myself if we didn't at least try to make it work.

"Not forever," Franck said. "Let's just give up for a few days. I propose we borrow my dad's car, go to Beaune, have a coffee, buy presents, and then eat and drink and try to forget the rest of it until Christmas is over."

I opened my mouth to protest, but in truth the image Franck painted was just too seductive. I twisted up my hair, slipped on my warmest sweater, and swiped on a coat of lip gloss I had found in the bottom of my backpack. Denial had an undeservedly bad reputation.

CHAPTER 14

The kitchen in Franck's parents' house smelled of snails. Well, not snails exactly. Snails don't actually smell like much all by themselves. But the way Mémé was preparing them, sautéed in parsley and garlic butter and then stuffed back into their shells, they smelled like heaven.

In the past four days we had managed to forget all about our house in a flurry of Christmas shopping, wrapping, and long frosty walks in the vineyards. We had just finished our last-minute shopping. The cold had taken grip in earnest while we had been fortifying ourselves post-shopping with stiff espressos at the Café Carnot. When we emerged, laden with wrapping paper and shopping bags, the cobblestones under our feet had become slippery with ice.

It felt like the whole world and everything in it, including myself, had fallen into an enchanted winter's sleep. Granted, since arriving at Franck's house to celebrate *Le Reveillon* with them, I had drunk two rather large glasses of *kir royale* - a regular *kir* that had been gussied up for the holidays by adding *crémant*, a bubbly champagne-style wine made in Burgundy – instead of the usual local white wine called *aligoté*.

Mesmerized by Mémé's deft movements, I watched as she assembled the French version of a Yule log. With her spatula she spread the *gateau de savoie* with her homemade chocolate *ganache*. She then rolled it up and wrapped the cake – which now resembled a very large sausage – in a damp tea towel she had prepared in advance. This accomplished, she peered into the oven where the *escargots* were bubbling away.

"You can't cook and do something else at the same time," she told me. Mémé had a penchant for doling out unsolicited advice, and never more so than when she was in what she called her *domaine*, the kitchen. "You need to keep an eye on things at all times. Even stopping to answer the phone can ruin everything."

I nodded. I was one of the only ones in the family who didn't tease Mémé when she gave advice, partly because I was brought up to be polite, and partly because I considered her instructions on life to be sound.

Her discourses tended to be on one of two subjects. The first was cooking, *bien sûr*. The second was men, philandering men like her first husband in particular. This specimen with a chronically wandering eye had been the father of Franck's two aunts (or his mother's half-sisters, technically). Even in France, where philandering was relatively commonplace, Mémé's first husband had been a philanderer beyond compare. One of the favourite family stories was that as he lay practically on his deathbed in the hospital, he was caught by his second wife with a hand up the skirt of one of the nurses.

Mémé always advised me that philandering men couldn't be changed: *"Quand ils sont comme ça, ils seront toujours comme ça."* When they are like that, she said, they will always be like that.

Mémé hadn't reacted to her first husband's philandering the way women were expected to do in the 1940s, which was simply to put up with it. On the day she found him reconnoitering with a fellow villager in the hayloft, she declared she had endured enough. She divorced him, moved to Villers-la-Faye and set herself up as the village *boulangère*. It required a stiff spine to withstand the whispers about her scandalous divorced background and her liberal ways. Still, her bread was delicious and the villagers came in droves. The villagers referred to Mémé as *la sauvage* or "the savage" because she seemed to have no need for any company besides that of her daughters and her own sisters and brothers.

That all changed when her first husband up and married one of his many paramours, a woman named Aline who, from that point onwards, became Mémé's nemesis. Aline became pregnant almost immediately. Mémé decided she had to get remarried too. She selected Georges, who lived across from the village bakery. They were married quickly and within months she was pregnant with Franck's mother.

The way she had lived took courage. When I was near Mémé, inhaling the scent of her cooking, I felt that somehow I was also soaking up some of her boldness.

Mémé pulled out a bubbling escargot from the oven and with her oven mitts placed it down on a little napkin in front of me.

"*Goûtez.*" She winked at me. "Tell me if you think they are ready."

At ten to eleven, after a feast of the delicious escargots and *foie gras* on tiny toasts with honeyed Sancerre wine, we staggered up the road toward the thundering bells of the village church. The midnight mass wasn't something Franck's parents – who had been very religious at one time but who had since become almost atheist – attended regularly, but Franck in particular had pushed for it this year. Even though I was usually no fan of church, given the state of our new home, prayer could hardly hurt.

Penetrating the inside of the church after walking through the silvery winter air was a shock. Inside, the temperature was roughly on par with Tahiti. I looked around and saw that the *Père Bard* had fitted out the church with six humongous heaters that emitted a burning stench reminiscent of the heaters at our new home.

We found seats together near the middle of the pews and underneath a swaying archway that seemed to have been constructed solely from dried vines and scotch tape. Cut out stars and drawings of the Virgin Mary made by the children hung down from these gravity-defying structures.

"I wonder how that thing is staying up?" I mused. I was sitting just underneath a Blessed Virgin who bore an uncanny resemblance to Pamela Anderson. She quivered in the tropical air. Baywatch had been a hit here in Burgundy too.

"Must be the Holy Spirit," Franck surmised.

A few raggedy hymns were sung and then the *Père Bard* eased his crooked body down on a rickety plastic chair that had been placed in the aisle between the two flanks of pews. He began to talk in that singsong tone of his and very quickly his sermon veered from the birth of Jesus to one of his favourite topics – the Blessed Virgin of Lourdes. For a non-Catholic, I knew an impressive amount about her. She just so happened to be a key figure in the lore of Franck's family. According to Michèle, who was paying close attention to *Le Père*, the Blessed Virgin of Lourdes was responsible for the existence of Franck's little brother Emmanuel-Marie, who sat perched like a blond cherub on my other side.

Michèle's brutal cancer treatment should have, according to every shred of medical evidence, rendered her sterile. Throughout her illness and her recovery she visited Lourdes several times and prayed to the Virgin. A few months after her treatment ended she began to have stomach-aches. Terrified that her cancer had metastasized she reluctantly booked an abdominal ultrasound. The doctor took his time in examining her. She was certain as she lay on the table that he was measuring new and inoperable tumors.

He finally wiped off the gel and announced cheerfully, "You will be feeling much better in seven months or so."

"Why? Will I be dead by then?" she asked.

He laughed and patted her shoulder. "*Non*. You'll have had your baby by then. You're around two months pregnant."

Unfortunately, when she shared her incredible news with her oncologist he was horrified. He was convinced that due to the extensive radiation she had endured, her baby would certainly be deformed and handicapped - if it survived at all. He urged her to have an abortion, or at least an amniocentesis. Michèle refused, unswerving in her belief that her baby was a miracle. Seven months later Emmanuel (meaning "God is with us") -Marie (to thank the Virgin) was born. He weighed in at over nine pounds and was perfectly healthy. Despite the fact that in the years following his arrival, Michèle and André had soured on the Catholic religion, the belief that the Virgin of Lourdes had played a part in Emmanuel-Marie's existence remained unassailable in Franck's family.

The *Père Bard* leaned forward on his cane, lowered his voice, and moved on to a different Virgin apparition - Our Lady of Fatima. I found myself leaning forward too. Apparently she had appeared in Portugal in 1917 and predicted the spread of communism, making prophesies about the annihilation of certain nations. *Père Bard* stood up shakily, galvanized by the topic. He began to thump his cane on the floor as he warned us all that we were going to die in a blaze of terror and flames, any day now.

I looked around me. This from a priest who, last time I had seen him, told me that God put us all here on earth to have fun. Emmanuel-Marie was fiddling with his hymnbook, the portly winemaker in front of me was picking the wax out of his ear, and Mémé was polishing the wooden pew with a corner of her shawl. Nobody was the slightest bit fazed.

"So what can one do?" the *Père Bard* asked, then looked out at his congregation. I listened carefully. I really wanted to know. *Le Père* turned his face up to the swaying arch that had miraculously, all stayed aloft. "All we can do is pray. *Tous ensemble*. Altogether, now."

He bowed his head, and I followed suit. If the end of the earth was truly imminent, that certainly put my house-related problems into perspective. Besides, it was comforting to feel for once as though I wasn't the only one who was doomed. We were all in this together. Maybe that feeling of not being alone was part of the reason why people had been coming to church for centuries.

In my head I asked the Virgin of Fatima and the Virgin of Lourdes and Jesus and God and basically whoever was listening for help, so that we could complete our renovations in time. I prayed that the neighbor wouldn't try to extort half of our house or kill Franck. I prayed that we would find a car (a cheap car, preferably). I prayed that I had made the right decision in leaving law and jumping into this house thing. And I prayed that somehow, even though I couldn't possibly see how from my current vantage point, everything would work out. After we had kissed our neighbours and walked back out into the winter air to the sound of church bells, I almost believed it could.

CHAPTER 15

Boxing Day isn't Boxing Day in France. It isn't a holiday at all, which is an oversight of epic proportions as anyone who has enjoyed a Christmas feast *à la française* needs a full two days to digest. In Franck's family, as with many other Burgundians, presents were small and secondary; the meal together was the true gift.

In Franck's house, the Christmas lunch went from half past eleven in the morning until nine o'clock at night. It included *escargots*, *foie gras* on little toasts with fig jam, paper thin slices of smoked salmon from Scotland, a roast turkey with chestnut and sausage stuffing, a huge cheese platter, and two *bûches de Noel*, one with chocolate ganache and the other with mocha butter cream. Plus there were after meal coffees and mandarin oranges and, last but not least, praline chocolates for those of us who hadn't already exploded.

Christmas Day really was a gift for me. For a full twenty-four hours, I managed to pretend that we had never bought the house at all and that we were just in Burgundy on a lovely vacation. I savoured every morsel of food and sip of wine that passed my lips, and the cashmere shawl of satisfaction they created.

There was no point in worrying anyway; we couldn't do anything until we had a car. That was on the agenda for the day after Christmas – the day that *wasn't* Boxing Day. Olivier had orchestrated the whole event. We were scheduled to meet with René in the town of Louhans, a market town in a region about an hour away called La Bresse. René worked there as a *garagiste* and was taking a day off to help us pick out a car.

I was shaken awake by Franck at six o'clock in the morning. We had a Spartan breakfast of big black bowls of coffee. Those *escargots* hadn't completely made their way down the digestive track yet and we didn't want to confuse them with any toasted slices of baguette. A few minutes later we set out in the dark to Louhans in André's car. Franck spent the drive telling me what I would be seeing if it was, in fact, daylight - pink and golden stone villages and rolling hills of the Côte D'Or giving way to flat farmland of La Bresse region. The houses in La Bresse were rambling one-level brick affairs built with deep eaves to shelter a multitude of drying cobs of corn. Part of me listened to his tour guide commentary, while part of me fretted about the probability of finding the right (meaning dirt cheap) car in a day.

The black sky paled to blue just as we entered the outskirts of Louhans. Franck rolled down his window and breathed in the cool air that was ripe with the smell of manure.

"*La vraie France!*" he declared.

This was confirmed by the river of berets and livestock and flowered pinafores which streamed by the window of the car as we entered town. Traffic slowed to a standstill; cows lowed in the distance.

"Is it always this busy?" I asked Franck as a man on foot with a crate of chickens hoisted on his shoulder weaved in front of us.

A beatific glow spread over Franck's features. "Monday is market day. Pépé Georges brought me here a few times when I was little." Franck, like his paternal grandfather, loved nothing better than a good French market. The ability to wile away a morning squeezing fruit while chatting to friends and strangers was imprinted in his DNA.

"But we're here to find a *car*," I reminded my husband. "Not go to a market." Franck didn't answer. Instead he watched with sparkling eyes as a man crossed the road in front of us with two goats in tow. "Where are we meeting René?" I asked with growing suspicion.

"At the market."

"You knew it was market day?" He had neglected to mention anything about that to me.

"*Bien sûr.* Monday is always market day in Louhans. Has been since the dawn of time."

I felt it best to clarify. "You agree that we are here to get a *car*, right?"

Franck tore his gaze from the livestock streaming by our car windows long enough to spare me an exasperated glance. "We have the whole day ahead of us Laura. Relax."

I loved markets, and I would have *loved* to relax, but I also knew my husband. Franck suffered from what I had loosely termed as "time dyslexia". In his mind, he could pack in a whole day's worth of activities between nine and ten o'clock in the morning. The car shopping was destined to get the short shift.

"We only have today - *one* day - to find a car."

"René is giving up his whole day to help us and Olivier told me he really wants to take us around the market first," Franck replied. "We can't be ungracious." Franck pulled an illegal U-turn and wedged the car into a tight parking spot just at the mouth of a narrow street thronging with people.

René was waiting for us. He leaned against the curved stone wall of the *rue principale*, which gave way to a covered passageway that ran down the entire length of the street as far as my eye could see. There was a matching passageway on the other side as well. The town had clearly been built with markets in mind.

René looked quite different than I had imagined. The knife-edge pleat down the front of his jeans was sharp enough to cut a round of *comté* and they were topped with a plaid dress shirt equally ironed within an inch of its life. He was smoking industriously. He changed his cigarette into his left hand in order to give Franck a manly shake with his right.

Franck's arm went around my shoulders. "Let me introduce you to Laura, *ma femme*."

René leaned down and gave me an enthusiastic kiss on each cheek. "This is your first time to Louhans, *n'est-ce pas?*"

"*Oui.*"

René's arm swept over the street and its beguiling passageways on either side. "Just look at those *arcades*! There are 157 in total. Louhans has one of the oldest preserved market *arcades* in all of France." That was an edifying fact, to be sure, but I was actually more interested in learning the number of used cars in Louhans.

Franck took his camera out of his backpack. When had he slipped that in? He began framing a photo.

René marched into the throng of market-goers and stands. "*Venez!*"

he beckoned to us. The scent of chicken manure and hay wafted over the cobblestones and René spouted facts like a seasoned tour guide. Without realizing it, I must have slowed down as we passed a table piled high with brightly coloured Emile Henry casserole dishes, Dutch ovens and pie pans.

"*Non, non, non,*" René tutted. "We can't start looking at things yet. It's strictly forbidden. "

"*Pourquoi?*"

"No decisions can be made until we've had our *petit blanc* and our *tête de veau.*"

Dread consumed me. I had tried to develop a taste for offal since falling in love with Franck, but so far it had proved to be an uphill battle. To me, kidneys smelled like hot urine, tripes tasted like *la merde,* and veal's head...I couldn't even wrap my mind around that one. Franck's eyes danced. *Tête de veau,* or veal's head, was one of his favorite meals, right up there with blood sausages and calves' liver.

René forged onwards until we popped out of the crowd and into a bistro packed with men wearing berets in every possible shade of indigo. Several wicker baskets containing chickens added an original note to the rumble of male conversation.

"I remember this place now! My *Pépé* used to bring me here." Franck breathed in the air thick with the smoke of *gauloises* cigarettes. I was one of only a handful of women in the place, and I was the only one who wasn't either wearing a flowered housedress or serving customers.

There wasn't an empty table in the place. Maybe we could forgo...

René weaved through the room to the smokiest table at the very back where two wizened men were nursing icy glasses of white wine. René nodded at them. "Do you mind?" he asked. The two men gave me a strange look, but after a moment one of them lifted his glass infinitesimally. Using his cigarette, René ushered Franck and me to sit down beside the men.

"I'm going to order for us." Before I could figure out a polite way to tell him that I didn't feel quite up to *tête de veau* at seven o'clock in the morning, René had been swallowed up by the crowd milling around the bar.

"What am I going to do?" I hissed at Franck in English. I didn't figure expressing my reservations in French would win me any popularity contests in this crowd. "I can't actually *eat* the stuff!"

"I wish I still smoked," he answered, surveying the room with a dreamy look.

René reappeared at our table with a carafe of white wine, the clear glass slick with condensation, and three glasses.

"Ladies first." He filled up a glass and handed it to me.

I took a sip. It was icy and delicious.

"This is what people drink here in the morning instead of coffee," René began, but was interrupted by the waitress who slung down three steaming platefuls of white, bumpy looking stuff on our table and a basket of sliced baguette. That cloying smell unique to innards hit my nostrils. My stomach lurched.

The wizened men beside us watched with growing respect. "*Bon Appétit.*" They lifted their glasses in a salute.

René picked up his fork and dug in. Franck quickly followed suit. I nibbled on a piece of baguette. Oh God, I just couldn't…but it would be so impolite to refuse…I took a few more gulps of wine.

The old men were watching me. I took a deep breath, scored one of the biggest pieces of white stuff with my fork, and slipped it in my mouth. I chewed. It was precisely the same consistency as something you would cough up at the tail end of a nasty case of bronchitis. I gagged as silently as possible.

Thankfully, René didn't look up but Franck arched a questioning eyebrow in my direction. I swallowed and gagged as discreetly as possible. With a feeling of impending doom, I forked another piece and repeated the same procedure, this time taking several gulps of wine to help it on its way down. It didn't help much. I did it again and again, but hardly seemed to be making a dent in my plateful of steaming veal's head. Franck's fork had been keeping pace with René's, but now he took it up a notch and polished off his plate with mind-boggling speed.

Then a man with the most florid nose I had ever seen tapped René's shoulder. René swivelled around in his chair; they shook hands, and launched into a conversation about the cow of somebody named Serge. Franck discreetly swapped his empty plate for my full one. I reached under the worn melamine table and squeezed his thigh in gratitude. I avoided looking at the men beside us.

After a minute or two, René and his acquaintance bid their *au revoirs* and René turned back to us and eyed our plates.

"Good work, Laura! There is nothing more charming than a woman with a good appetite." He eyed Franck's plate, which my husband had already almost emptied. "What's wrong? Don't you like it?"

Franck shrugged off the notion with disdain. I'm just savouring every mouthful," he said.

CHAPTER 16

More than an hour later, and after a second carafe of white wine and a round of stiff espressos, René led us out of the bistro. Now that we had honored the breakfast traditions of Louhans, he would surely lead us to a car lot.

Like a raging river, the market mob carried us to a crosswalk commandeered by a majestic *gendarme* kitted out in a winter cape and square hat. He ushered us across, stopping oncoming cars with the sheer force of his sartorial splendour. We found ourselves on the other side of the road in a large square which, according to the blue enamel sign, was called *Place de la Charité*.

"Now are we going to look for a car?-" I began to ask.

Franck's shoe came down hard on my foot. René flicked his cigarette.

"A car! That is easy. The perfect chicken...now *there* is a challenge."

"A chicken?" I made the mistake of asking.

"Do not think you are in the presence of just any *poulet!*" he remonstrated, and proceeded to lead us on a circumambulation of the stands. Apparently, we were in the presence of the world's only blue-footed chickens known as *poulet de bresse*. These pampered specimens were prized amongst chefs and French people from all walks of life including, it seemed, *garagistes*.

"Many believe that their unrivalled taste comes from the fact that the soil around here is lacking in calcium which makes their bones unusually fine," René said. "Me, I am convinced that it is because they are fed only milk, sweet corn, and other hand-picked grains." René stopped in his tracks, struck by a particularly plump specimen. He lifted its red wattles, ran a practised hand over the white feathers, and inspected its feet, which were indeed the same shade of indigo as the well-worn berets in the bistro.

René began to debate with the chicken's equally robust owner who was dressed in a blinding fuchsia and orange patterned housecoat under her wool jacket. I glanced at my watch. Ten o'clock already. I wanted to be negotiating cars, not chickens. Besides, what was René going to do with a live chicken? Use it in some voodoo ceremony to help us decide on a vehicle?

I gave Franck a nudge and tapped my watch pointedly. He shrugged. He couldn't, however, hide the shine in his eyes. He was enjoying himself. Immensely.

I had never been blessed with a patient nature, and my stint at Oxford had only compounded the problem. In the past two years, I had been so hard pressed to get my weekly reading and essays completed that I had to stay up two to three nights a week just to be able to get all the work done. Any minute spent doing something unproductive filled every cell of my being with guilt. Even now, this meandering through the day when we had something urgent to do made an invisible iron band tighten around my chest. I had to remind myself to breathe. Black dots danced in front of the white plumage of the chicken René was extorting me to admire.

I must have been looking as distracted as I felt, because René firmly pulled me closer and lifted my hand so that I could feel the glossiness of the chicken's feathers for myself.

"This is the one," he announced.

I eyed the chicken, who eyed me back with a knowing look. "*Très jolie,*" I agreed without enthusiasm.

René pointed his cigarette at me. "You're not looking, Laura. *Really* look." Shame washed over me. If the chickens were this important to René I had to at least make an effort. "She will be my gift to you," René added.

"*Quoi!?*" The word popped out of my mouth, incredulous, before I could stop myself. "But I…we…can't accept it. You shouldn't be buying us gifts when you have already agreed to take your day off and help us. Besides…how would we carry it?"

The seller held up an empty crate from behind her stall and offered to give it to us for free.

"There you go!" René patted my arm. "Everything has a way of working out, *n'est-ce pas?*"

"I would have no idea what to do with a live chicken!"

The woman narrowed her eyes at me, and then turned them accusingly on René for foisting such an incompetent on her. She pulled the chicken back to the safety of her fuchsia housecoated protection. "You wouldn't know how to cook her?" she demanded.

"I would," Franck said. "My grandmother used to make *poulet de bresse au vin jaune et morilles* all the time. She used to flambé it in *Calvados* - what is your opinion on that?"

The chicken's owner visibly softened. She enlightened Franck on why *Calvados* should never be employed, but solely *vin jaune*, or yellow wine from the Jura region.

René beamed.

"Franck, do you also know how to butcher a chicken?" I asked pointedly. Franck shot me a dirty look. The seller arched a brow, waiting for his answer.

"Not really," he admitted. The woman removed the empty crate she had deposited on the counter and muttered something in unintelligible *patois*.

"My wife is right," Franck said. "We would botch up the butchering. We're all but camping in our house as it is now. We don't even have the correct knives."

"Don't you worry." She smiled at Franck's obvious regret and pulled out a knife capable of terrorizing a pirate from underneath her housedress. "I'll butcher her for you. She won't be quite as good as freshly butchered, but it will still be better than any chicken you'll find elsewhere."

René clapped my shoulder. "When should we come and pick her up?"

"In about an hour or so," she said, pursing her lips. She took out a whetstone and began to sharpen her knife.

"Perfect," René said. "That will give us just enough time to choose a rabbit."

"I could use a *petit café*," René mused after our interminable visit to the rabbit section on the far side of the Place de la Charité.

We somehow managed to dissuade René from buying us a rabbit, but instead of being disappointed he was much refreshed from an edgy debate with one of the rabbit vendors during which both parties insulted each other's intelligence and eyesight, all while addressing each other in formal "*vous*". It ended in a cordial handshake and a promise from René to return without fail and visit the seller at next Monday's market. By the end, I was hopping from one foot to the other with impatience.

We followed René again as he plunged us back into the heart of the narrow market street. We resurfaced in a 1900s-era café with scarred wooden tables and chairs polished by decades of elbows and *derrières*. René ordered three espressos then settled down beside Franck and me with a satisfied sigh.

"This is my favorite café," he said. I took in the patina of the painted panels that ran up to the thirteen or fifteen foot ceiling. It was stunning, but I was far too annoyed to admit that. We sat in the café for about an hour after we had finished our espressos. René chatted with acquaintances who came and went while I fidgeted and tried to keep a lid on my temper. The day was almost half gone and we hadn't even begun to *look* for a car. Without a car we couldn't begin our renovations. Our first guests arrived in four months. How could Franck just sit there, looking so content?

At long last René consulted his watch. "Your chicken! We have to go and pick it up."

On the way back through the throng to pick up our chicken, I felt a surge of optimism – stalls were being dismantled, the market was drawing to a close. With any luck, the woman would be gone by the time we got back to the *place* and so would our chicken.

We passed by the stand I had seen earlier with the towering Emile Henry cookware. "Factory Seconds," the sign read. "Today only." An amazing mixing bowl caught my eye – big enough for cookie dough or even a massive summer salad. It was cornflower blue with the purest white inside. Without realizing it I had slowed down.

René held his arm out and stopped us. "You like that?"

"She loves Emile Henry," Franck answered for me.

"I do but I have nowhere to put anything right now anyway. You should see our kitchen."

"There is always a place for something we truly love." René sallied up to the seller and introduced himself. They chatted for a bit while I examined a cobalt quiche dish and a sunflower yellow *terrine*, but my hands kept going back, running themselves over the cool surface of the blue bowl.

"Show me which things you like," René instructed.

"This bowl is really nice," I murmured. I couldn't seem to let go of it.

"It's your colour," Franck said. "Buy it."

"Wait, wait, wait!" René held up his hand. "How much?" he asked the vendor, and then proceeded in a lively and lengthy negotiation that sliced the initial asking price in half. My eyes alighted on six cherry red ramekins.

After half an hour of negotiations, chatting, and choosing, we made our way back to André's car, René and Franck staggering under the weight of my purchases. With the exception of knives and forks, I had completely outfitted our new kitchen at *La Maison des Deux Clochers*. Maybe we didn't have a car, but we did have a lemon yellow terrine dish, those adorable red ramekins, two cobalt casserole dishes, a lime green pie plate, and my treasured cornflower bowl - and, thanks to René, all of it came at a ridiculously low price.

We had filled the trunk of Franck's father's car and had just managed to shut the hatch when René slapped his forehead.

"Your chicken!"

Franck and I raced after him through the thinning market thoroughfare and back out to *La Place de la Charité*. I felt a curious sensation in my chest, like a shiny soap bubble about to burst. The sensation was strangely similar to the anxiety that had become such a constant companion, yet also completely different. I felt a kinship with the other market goers and the beautiful cobbled street, and even René.

I was having fun. The realization hit me as we caught sight of our chicken's seller packing up her table.

"I had taken you for lost," she said, crossing her arms across her majestic bosom. "I had decided to eat this pretty beast for lunch, but seeing as you are here now..."

She handed Franck a brown paper package tied together with twine. He took it as carefully as you would a newborn baby.

"*Merci.*" René was still gulping for air. "You see we were buying some bowls and we got talking..."

She twitched a shoulder. "It happens." René began to peel French francs out of his wallet.

"We can't let you pay for it," I said. I opened my bag but René pushed my money away.

"*Non, non, non.* It must be my treat." He looked so insulted that I blushed and slid my wallet back.

"Then you must let us treat you to lunch,' Franck said.

René thoughtfully patted his non-existent gut. "I *am* getting hungry." A new gleam flashed in his eyes. "I know the perfect place!"

Within ten minutes René, Franck, the butchered blue-footed chicken, and I were ensconced in a snug table at the local *routier* – the French version of a truck stop.

"Where are the menus?" I asked after the waitress deposited a huge glass bottle of red wine on the red gingham tablecloth beside a basket full of chopped up baguette and another carafe filled with water.

"There are no menus at *routiers*," Franck reminded me. "You just get whatever they feel like cooking."

"It's always delicious," René assured me. "Just last week I had the most amazing *andouilettes* here."

Andouillettes were one of Franck's favorite things in the world. They were sausages made of pigs' intestines. They smelled like a cow pie and I couldn't imagine they tasted any better. Please God, no.

René served me a large glass of wine and I took a big gulp.

The patroness came out of the kitchen bearing three steaming plates. It didn't smell like offal. I almost crowed with relief when she set my plate down. Tomatoes. Stuffed tomatoes, or *tomates farcies*, to be exact. I picked up my fork and dug in. The meat was a succulent mix of sausage and beef infused with the tomato juice. They were served with rice which soaked up the delectable sauce.

Just when I thought that my bliss couldn't be more profound, the patroness replaced our clean plates with steaming plates of stewed rabbit and prunes in a white wine sauce. It was so succulent that if the market hadn't been over I would have seriously considered going back and buying a rabbit of our own.

Next came a huge platter of cheeses, then an individual *crème brûlée* for each of us, and finally, of course, an espresso with a perfect little piece of dark chocolate.

René's flow of anecdotes and stories washed over me like soothing music. I watched the other tradesmen come and go until we had been the last people in the restaurant for quite some time.

"I wonder what time it is?" Franck asked, though his tone suggested that he didn't much care.

"No idea," I murmured. Even though I was wearing a watch – I always wore a watch – it seemed like too much effort to check it.

René checked his. "It's three o'clock. What time did you have to get back?"

"My dad needs the car by five," Franck said, and sat up a little straighter. "It will take us at least an hour to get back. Do we have time to look at a few cars before we go?"

"Maybe a few," René said. "Come on."

An hour later we had to conclude that the car part of our day had been just as unsuccessful as the market portion of our day had been successful. René had taken us to the garage where he worked and, in a desultory fashion, showed us the two used cars that were parked out back. We would have taken either one for the right price, but after giving them a thorough once-over, René deemed them both pieces of junk. I tried to assure him that neither Franck nor I were at all averse to pieces of junk, but René proved stubborn.

Franck reached over and checked my watch. "We have to go if we're going to get back in time."

"That was a fine day!" René remarked as he helped Franck rearrange our purchases in the back of the car.

"It was a fine day," I agreed. "Thank you." I tried to muster up a little disappointment about not finding a car but it proved impossible with the memory of our lunch and the Emile Henry haul fresh in my mind. René grasped me by the shoulders and planted a hearty kiss on each cheek.

"*Au revoir.*" He passed me our chicken as I climbed into André's car. As Franck turned the engine René leaned down to my open window.

"Remember Laura" - he tapped on the roof twice - "never confuse what is urgent with what is truly important."

CHAPTER 17

I woke up the next morning turning over René's parting words in my mind. They had been a revelation yesterday evening after our *routier* lunch and a significant quantity of the house red, but now I felt more muddled than ever. How was I supposed to know the difference between what was urgent and what was important? Getting the car was urgent, but it had also been important - hadn't it? The chicken which was now safely entrusted into Mémé's capable hands had been important, of course, but it still didn't change the fact that we were stranded in Magny-les-Villers without a car.

I pulled on my clothes and tried to make a mental list of important things in my life while I heated up a saucepan of milk and turned on the coffee. Franck, of course. Our families, for sure. Delicious food. Good wine also deserved a top spot. I ran my finger over my new blue bowl, slowing down over the splash of blue paint on the white. It felt important. Wait - that was ridiculous. It was a salad bowl for goodness sake.

I drank my *café au lait*, picked up my wallpaper stripper and trudged back into the bedrooms to continue stripping the walls. I had felt more triumph in finding my salad bowl than I had when I learned I had earned a 2:1 in my law finals. How could *that* be?

Franck came in quite a while later after smoothing things over with his parents about the car, or rather our continued lack of one.

"I've got an idea," he said.

"About what?" I asked.

"Our car."

Another big chunk of plaster fell on the floor beside me. I had gotten used to this and just threw it into my pail and kept on working. "Let's hear it."

"*Alors*...the thing is, I know somebody in Chalon. Somebody who sells cars." There was an odd note of hesitation in his voice. I shifted around to get a better look at my husband.

"Why didn't we go and see this person to begin with?"

Franck squinted at a hole in the plaster.

"An ex-girlfriend?" I guessed. It wouldn't be the first time I was brought face to face with one of Franck's numerous ex-girlfriends. Girls had caught Franck's interest at an early age, ten to be exact. We routinely stumbled over Franck's ex-girlfriends when we were in Burgundy, but I was secretly thankful he wasn't the type of man who stayed friends with them after breaking up.

"Not exactly," he mumbled. "He is the father of an ex-girlfriend."

"Which ex-girlfriend?" I was not a jealous person by nature, but some ex-girlfriends definitely counted more than others. "Have I met her?"

"Juliette."

My heart sank. She wasn't AN ex-girlfriend - she was THE ex-girlfriend.

Juliette grew up in the neighboring village of Meuilley and she and Franck went out for three years. They broke up about eight months before Franck and I met; Stéphanie had told me that after the rupture Franck remained holed up in his bedroom with the an enormous pile of philosophy books and tried to commit metaphorical suicide by overdosing on Nietzsche and Sartre. It was only a summons from the *Président de la République* himself in the form of a letter saying that Franck had to report for his mandatory military service that finally dislodged him from his refuge. He was legally obliged to emerge from his room, get a buzz cut, and rejoin the human race.

I met Juliette just before I left France at the end of my exchange year, in a café just off the *rue de la Liberté* in Dijon. Franck had brought me there because he was giving me a tour of his favorite haunts from his university days. I had my hair twisted back and anchored messily with a tortoise-shell barrette and wore a chiffon scarf with little light blue flowers all over it tied nonchalantly around my neck. The spring air was magical and I was feeling very much in love.

Franck settled me at a table by the window then went to the bar to order our espressos. I played with the sugar packets for a while but when I looked up for Franck I was startled to see he was talking earnestly to a woman. Her back was turned but I noticed her blond hair waved most of the way down a narrow, graceful back. She was shaking her head but Franck nodded, insistent. I had no idea who she was; however, I did find myself hoping to discover that when she turned around she had a low forehead and a moustache.

Just then she did. No such luck. Franck prodded her and she stalked resentfully over to where I was sitting. I turned my face up to Franck in question. Franck set our coffees on the table but remained standing, his face grim but determined.

Her aquamarine eyes examined me. They were set in a perfect oval face that was set off by full, beautifully shaped lips. White-hot envy shot through me.

"Laura," Franck said. "I'd like you to meet Juliette. Juliette, this is my girlfriend, Laura."

My heart contracted like a sea anemone poked with a stick, but I could *not* let it show. I stood up and leaned over to give her an awkward *bises*. I bumped the table and scalding espresso sloshed down one leg of my white jeans. Juliette stared at the spreading stain, mumbled something, then kissed Franck on the cheek and hurried away.

I collapsed back into my chair.

"Are you burnt?" Franck snatched up a napkin and rubbed my leg.

"*That* was Juliette?" A minute ago I had felt beautiful. Now…

Franck brushed a finger across my blazing cheek. "Does it hurt very much?"

"I'm fine," I lied. As fine as a hedgehog beside a unicorn could ever feel, that is to say, not very fine at all.

"I'm relieved Juliette has met you now," Franck said. "That should be the end of that."

"The end of *what*?" I fought for breath.

Franck stirred his espresso. "She has been phoning me and saying she wants to get back together." I wanted to curl up in a ball but I forced myself to sit up straighter.

"And?" I asked.

Franck looked up at me. The clanking of the coffee cups and the murmur of conversation at the bar seemed very far away.

"How could you even ask that?" he said. "I have told her that I am not interested. I told her that I am in love with you."

I reached over, twisted his T-shirt in my hand and kissed him. Relief coursed through my veins. It hit me then how what had begun as an exotic whirlwind romance had deepened into something else entirely. If I lost him, I knew I would regret it for a very long time. Maybe forever.

Even now that we were married, the mere mention of Juliette had the power of hurtling me back in time so that I felt exactly like that eighteen year old sitting in that smoky café. Especially now, when I was covered with plaster dust and feeling somewhat lost in my own life.

"Her father is really nice." Franck picked up another scraper lying on the floor and knelt down beside me. "I always got along with him." He began to scrape slowly, thoughtfully. "I don't want to have to ask to borrow my parents' car again; I think we can borrow Stéph's today. She's off work." I knew Franck was waiting to hear my decision.

"Do you want to go now?" I asked. "If we can borrow her car maybe we can go and see Juliette's father before lunch."

Franck dropped the scraper and went off in search of the phone.

Thirty minutes later, I was in Chalon shaking Juliette's father's hand.

"Please, call me Antoine," he said. He had sparkling aquamarine eyes like his daughter and professed to be enchanted to finally meet me. Juliette was of course mentioned, but just a quick update that she was living in Lyon now with a boyfriend named Giles.

In a stark contrast to René, Antoine quickly brought the conversation back around to the subject of the kind of car we were looking to purchase. While Franck filled him in, he led us outside to the lot at the back of his dealership. We began looking at price tags. Everything was light-years beyond our budget.

"What is your budget exactly?" Antoine asked finally.

He paled when Franck named a figure, but led us to the very back of the lot where there were four vehicles that had clearly seen better days. Antoine led us right to the worst one in the lot — a white car speckled with spots of rust peeping through the flaking white paint.

"A Renault 21," Antoine tapped the hood. "Doesn't look like much and she has lot of kilometers on her but I think she will hold up for you" — he frowned - "for a few months anyway."

"How much?" Franck asked. A half an hour later, we were signing the purchase papers.

"You see?" Franck tapped Stéphanie's steering wheel after we had arranged to pick up our car the next morning. "Everything works out in the end. Now we don't only have a car, but we are going back to my parents to feast on a delicious chicken for lunch. *Elle n'est pas belle la vie?* Isn't life beautiful?"

As we wound up through the vineyards on our way back to Magny-les-Villers, it did seem that my chronic attempts to control the future were unnecessary. After all, Franck and I had managed to stay together and even get married despite the ravishing Juliette. If I just relaxed, maybe both the urgent and the important and everything else would take care of itself. We had an epic task ahead of us in the months to come. I would have to remind myself often that in looking for a car, we ended up with not only a car but also a delicious chicken lunch and a pile of gorgeous Emile Henry tableware. On that gray December day, *la vie* did seem *belle* indeed.

After the excitement of the chicken expedition combined with the heady possession of our new car, Franck and I seemed to be stuck in the monotony of scraping off every inch and every layer of wallpaper throughout the house. The world outside seemed to grind to a halt, suspended by the frost. The temperature had plummeted and villagers were saying this would be one of the hardest winters of the last fifty years.

The days took on a routine. We woke up shivering, showered in the cold, scraped off wallpaper in the cold until we got down to the crumbling plaster, and then went to bed in the cold. I asked myself several times a day what the hell we were doing. Progress seemed slow and, at times, virtually non-existent.

"We need to get someone to help us with the re-plastering," Franck moaned as yet another chunk of the wall disintegrated between his fingers. "I should call Olivier and see if he's thought of anybody."

I had no patience for all this waiting around to see if other people could help us. We should be able to figure this out on our own. I scraped harder and the plaster crumbled down, making a huge hole between the big old wooden baseboard and the wall above.

"Don't forget that we don't even own the whole place yet." I tightened in resentment at this fact. "You'd better make a phone call to the surveyor while you're at it."

"He's scheduled to come in two days," Franck reminded me.

"You could call and confirm." When was Franck going to start to expect the worst rather than naïvely hope for the best? We'd never get the house done if we kept doing things his way.

"I think he needs to be harassed," I said. "You need to be more on top of things like that."

My tendency to blame others when things weren't going well had never made me proud. It was brought to my notice for the first time in grade three, the year I had Mrs. Lusk for my teacher. She had feathered black hair and wore A-line skirts with nude nylons and wedge sandals. I idolized her. She loved art projects and was very excited to teach us all how to make our very own macramé plant hanger. We were paired up in teams and took turns holding the strings tight while the other person wove them together like Mrs. Lusk had showed us. Lisa, my partner, wove her hanger with deft fingers. Mrs. Lusk made the entire class stop their weaving and have a look at the marvel Lisa had produced.

My cheeks burned. I was going to do better. My weaving would be so brilliant that Mrs. Lusk was going to stop the entire class and exclaim about my plant hanger too. She would announce that I was far more talented than Lisa.

When it finally came my turn to weave, my fingers didn't seem to work properly. The strands kept slipping away from me as sweat started to bead on my forehead. In the end, my plant hanger was a distinctly lumpy, ugly affair.

"It's nice," lied Lisa. I shot her a look of pure hatred.

Mrs. Lusk came by just as I was fretfully trying to untie and retie the three end pieces together. She placed a gentle hand on my shoulder. "I think maybe you didn't knot your strands tight enough, Laura."

This wasn't happening the way it was supposed to happen. She was supposed to notice how wonderful I was, not how hopeless. I couldn't stand her thinking badly of me.

"Lisa didn't hold the strands properly," I said. I felt both relieved and ashamed as soon as the words came out of my mouth.

Mrs. Lusk kneeled down so that her feathered hair brushed my arm. "Laura, it is a very bad habit to blame other people for our own difficulties."

My innards curled up in mortification. Since that day I had been painfully aware of this nasty tendency to blame others when I was doing or feeling badly. I resisted most of the time, but the worse I felt, the stronger my urge to blame someone for it... like now.

"I can't believe you haven't called *Le Maître* about that mistake in the plan again," I snapped at Franck. "Besides, why did we use him as a notary in the first place? You knew he was an incompetent drunk."

Franck stood over me, picking off the gluey bits of plaster that were stuck to the end of his scraper. "The one time we tried to find a different notary he cheated us out of a house, or have you forgotten that already?" His voice was as icy as the road outside our window.

"You give up too easily." I threw down the scraper, rage boiling up inside me. "You're just not persistent enough."

In Canada, or even in England, I would have been on the phone harassing the *cadastre* until he did something but I knew that in France things didn't work like that. This was, of course, because the French did not operate on the premise that the client was always right. In fact, a French person would have no compunction about hanging up on a client – repeatedly, if necessary. Franck had told me time and time again that what was needed to get things done in France was summarized in one word - seduction. The trick was getting people to like you enough that they wanted to help you. Franck was a million times better at this than I was, but feeling useless just stoked my anger.

"You give up too easily," I muttered again.

"You blame people too easily," Franck said, his eyes kindling.

He was right and I knew it, but my fury had nowhere else to go. I threw my scraper down on the wood floor. "Screw this. I'm going for a walk."

Franck glanced past me to the window. "It's snowing."

"I'm not blind."

I pulled on my boots and jacket and stormed out the door. A blast of air that must have blown right off the Siberian plains hit my face. I almost stopped but my pride wouldn't let me. I shuffled up the icy road as quickly as I could until I reached the far wall of the church across the street. I pressed my body as far as it would go into the nook where the wall of the vestry met the wall of the nave. The cold of the stone seeped quickly into my flushed skin. Why hadn't I stopped long enough to put on gloves, a scarf and my wool hat? I stamped my feet and tried to shove tighter in the corner. *Merde* it was cold.

Maybe I could walk but where would I go? It was pitch dark and probably ten degrees below zero. I could sneak inside the church; it would be warmer in there. Not a lot, but it would be protected from the wind anyway.

I peeked around the wall. I could make out Franck's silhouette as he watched out the living room window. Why didn't he come out to find me? I had enough sense of self-preservation not to go and throw myself in a ditch and freeze to death, but the fact that he knew that was highly annoying. I couldn't feel my fingers anymore.

We hadn't fought like this in a very long time. During our two years in Oxford we hardly ever fought. Then again, we hardly saw each other either. Our lives just hadn't intersected very much besides a few brief moments of overlap. Those were snatches when I wasn't buried under a pile of law books or Franck wasn't spending the week in Versailles taking photos of French film stars that would end up in the next issue of Paris Match.

Now I had pitchforked the two of us into this house mess that promised to be every bit as stressful as law school. Why did things always have to be so difficult and complicated? I had spent my adult years searching for the magic key that would make my life effortless, the way it seemed for so many other people, yet it continued to elude me.

This house project was supposed to bring Franck and me closer than ever before, but now I realized that it was just as likely to drive us even further apart.

My fingers were stiff and I couldn't jam them any further in the fleece of my jacket pockets. I couldn't unknot the tangle of my thoughts or resolve our multitude of renovation woes either, but I could go back inside so that Franck wouldn't be worried. Hopefully, he was a *little* bit worried by now.

I emerged from my hiding spot into the howling wind and slid down the road toward the house. Shame burned a bright spot in each of my otherwise numb cheeks. I slunk up the stairs into the warmth of the veranda.

Before I could turn its worn knob, Franck opened the big wooden door from the other side, pulled me against his chest, and enveloped me in a crushing hug. The scent of plaster dust and apples was deeply ingrained in the scratchy wool of his sweater. He plucked off my hat and buried his face into my hair.

"I was just coming to get you," he murmured.

"I'm sorry," I mumbled. "I don't know why I got mad like that...I didn't mean to...I am just so..."

Franck squeezed me tighter against him. "I know. You're still a mess."

I nodded. "I'm sorry I worried you."

"I wasn't worried. I saw you go behind the church. I knew you'd come back when you got cold enough."

I opened my mouth but then shut it again. I deserved that. "Why were you coming to get me then?"

"To tell you that I just got off the phone with the *cadastre*, who *did* call me back. He's coming in a week."

Here I was, knowing I needed to reconnect with Franck after two years of distance and yet sabotaging that very goal with my impatience and control-freak tendencies. I was sick of acting so unlovably. "I'm sorry I yell - "

"Then Olivier called me."

"*Alors?*"

"He invited us over for coffee right now. His friend Le Gégé has dropped by and he might be able to help us."

That was the best piece of news I'd heard in a long time. I looked down at my icy boots.

"Does it worry you that we're fighting so much?" I asked in a quiet voice.

Franck twisted a stray bit of hair that had slipped out of my ponytail around his wrist. "*Non*. It worries me when we never fight at all, like in Oxford."

I looked up into his face and traced the curve of his quirked lips with my finger. Franck never failed to surprise me with his unique way of looking at the world. "You must be feeling very reassured these days then."

Franck kissed the cold tip of my nose. "Very."

CHAPTER 18

I was barely in the door of Olivier's house when he thrust a glass of *kir* in my hand. His face bore a knowing, compassionate look that reminded me of a Gallic, barrel-chested Dalai Lama.

I gave Dominique *les bises* and tried to give Marcel one on his head of curls, but he ran away from me, shrieking with laughter. I spotted a slight, young looking but balding man bending through the low doorway that led from the kitchen area to the large living room of Olivier's house. A cigarette dangled from his lips.

"The floor is poured too thick," he said to no-one in particular.

Franck strode towards him and extended his hand. "Gégé. *Ça va?*"

Gégé's eyes crinkled in a way that was both shy and friendly at the same time. He shook Franck's hand. "Ah, *Le Fou*," he mused. "Olivier has been telling me about this ruin you bought. Sounds like you're as crazy as ever, *hein?*"

Franck and his village buddies all had nicknames growing up. Franck had been christened *Le Fou* or "The Crazy One", no doubt due to his penchant for doing things like deciding late into a party one night that he was going to drive down to Monaco in time to see the sun rise over the Mediterranean.

Franck introduced me. Gégé stuck out his hand to shake but I had already leaned in to give him the *bises*. He blushed but didn't seem displeased.

"We need to go back in the living room," he collared Olivier who had tried to sit back down at the kitchen table. "I need to tell you everything you did wrong." Olivier expelled a put-upon sigh, but he got up and followed us through the low stone doorway.

"Franck deserves his share of the blame too," Olivier grumbled. "After all, he helped me pour the floor."

"Don't worry," Gégé said. "I'll shame him too."

It didn't seem prudent to mention that I had actually watched the pouring of the floor we now stood upon. That day was stamped in my memory. Olivier had enlisted Franck and Martial and a few other stalwart and muscular friends to pour a concrete slab in the huge upper floor of the barn so that he could transform it into a massive living area. It just so happened that the pour was scheduled for two days before I was due to go back to Canada. I remember watching as Franck shovelled the heavy concrete from a wheelbarrow and paused only occasionally to turn his head and cast me a secret smile. I stored each one up like a precious jewel. I was starting university in Montreal in the fall and I didn't know when, or even if, I would ever see Franck again.

The consensus amongst Franck's friends and family here in Burgundy was that it was a long shot. Franck was twenty-three, just finishing his mandatory military service, had no money, and had never been on an airplane in his life. I was eighteen and was slotted to begin my Bachelor of Arts at McGill. Our future lives ran in parallel rather than intersecting streams. By sheer force of will we bent our paths until they intersected.

Olivier had similarly twisted his destiny. When his friends poured this massive floor for him they had all wondered, Franck included, why a single man like Olivier would need all that extra space in his new house. The old man who had lived in this house before him had been an inveterate bachelor, or *vieux garçon*. When Mémé heard the news that Olivier had bought this house she wrung her dishtowel in her hands and declared that by buying the house Olivier was damning himself to the same fate.

Luckily Olivier hadn't listened to whispers. Before the floor had fully cured, Olivier met his future wife Dominique, and their son Marcel was born just a year later. Sometimes I wondered if by pouring this floor Olivier hadn't actually paved the way to a new life for himself.

I liked to believe that people could change the course of their lives. That's sort of what I had been trying to do, albeit in a floundering way, when we had bought *La Maison des Deux Clochers*. It hadn't gone exactly as planned so far, but maybe Gégé could help us turn things around.

But not yet. At that moment he was pointing at the massive crack in the plaster of the wall that ran from the floor (now tiled over the concrete) to the huge oak beams about fifteen feet above our heads.

"You used too much concrete for the subfloor." Gégé cast both Franck and Olivier a withering look. "Its weight is causing the walls to crack."

Olivier narrowed his eyes at Franck who, judging from his twitching lips, appeared to be fighting back a smile. "How did we calculate the thickness Franck?" he asked. "I can't remember."

"We didn't," Franck said. "But I do remember that we tried to make you a nice, thick floor - better than having you fall through to the cellar below."

Gégé snorted. "Little risk of that. *Par contre*. As for the walls caving in…"

"I don't want my walls to fall in!" Olivier cried. "What can I do? There must be something. Stop torturing me, Gégé." For all his Oracle-like ways, Olivier was very quick to alarm.

"I think he's enjoying torturing you," Franck observed. Gégé inclined his head, acknowledging this truth. He then took several thoughtful drags on his cigarette, milking Olivier's panic for all it was worth.

"A steel beam," he pronounced, at last.

Olivier groaned. "Where?"

"In the cellar to support the floor. It needs to run under its whole length. Then you'll have to plaster up that crack. "

"Can you do that?" Olivier said. My heart leapt. Given the state of our walls, if we were lucky enough to find a plasterer…"

"*Non*, not me," Gégé said. "Plastering requires real skill, but I have a friend who might help."

Olivier waved us back towards the kitchen. "There is a lot to discuss. We need another drink."

Once we were seated around the kitchen table again, second *kir* in hand and the beam fully debated, Olivier said to Franck, "I've been telling Le Gégé about your little problem."

"Doesn't sound so little," Gégé noted.

I thought briefly of playing down the bind we had gotten ourselves into, but then realized that if we were lucky enough to get Gégé in the door, he would be seeing it all for himself.

"To be honest, I wonder now if we were crazy to buy the house," I admitted.

"I'm sure Franck made you do it." Gégé tapped the side of his head with his cigarette. "He's always been crazy. Can't believe you married him. Perhaps you're a little crazy too?"

Franck seemed pleased rather than offended by this observation and went on to recount in horrific detail our rotting, humid walls, the turquoise bathroom fixtures, and our mysterious lack of hot water. He paused for a moment after this edifying description, during which time my heart seemed to stop. Only a masochist would sign up for such a project.

"Want in?" Franck asked, as though he were offering Gégé a rare treat.

Gégé stubbed out his cigarette and lit another one. The church bell rang the seven o'clock *angelus* which lasted a good five minutes. I began to wonder if Gégé had heard Franck's question. Finally, his shoulders twitched infinitesimally.

"*Pourquoi pas?*" he said.

"What?" I asked, not sure I trusted my ears. "You want in?"

"Is it a hopeless cause?" Gégé asked.

Franck and I exchanged a glance. "Yes," we admitted.

Gégé smiled. "In that case, I'm in."

The next day was *Le Réveillon*, or New Year's Eve. Gégé hadn't given us any idea when he would appear but we both clung to the hope he would materialize on our doorstep sooner rather than later. We waited all day for the sound of his footsteps on our massive stone staircase, but they never came.

Franck and I didn't have the budget or the heart to go out and celebrate, so instead we made a foray into Nuits-Saint-Georges and sprung for a rabbit-eared antenna for the ancient black and white TV that we had unearthed from the depths of the buffet. Franck uncorked a bottle of 1985 *Corton-Charlemagne* that his uncle Georges had given him for his twentieth Birthday. We sipped it out of Duralex kitchen glasses while we watched the dancers of the Crazy Horse revue direct from Paris on our dusty sofa bed. The stunning dancers looked grainy – our reception was far from perfect – but we could make out their perky bare breasts and their glinting sequins and the audience, chicly dressed and swilling *Dom Pérignon*. We could not have stumbled upon anything farther removed from our current and decidedly unglossy reality.

Even so, there was something satisfying about spending New Year's Eve together in a disintegrating house. Previously, celebrating New Year's had always felt forced to me. We usually ended up at one party or another but I always felt pressured to have a marvellous time when in fact, all I really wanted to do was go home and curl up on the couch with a good book. Trying to orchestrate joy, like I did most on New Year's, always backfired. Joy seemed to prefer sneaking up and pouncing on me where it was least expected.

It had been that way on our New Year's the year Franck and I lived in Paris. I was studying Medieval French at the Sorbonne for my third year of university and Franck was working as a journalist at a magazine called *Expo News*. We had made epic plans for New Year's Eve – meeting up with friends of mine from Canada in Edinburgh to celebrate Hogmanay, the raucous Scottish celebration of New Year's that involves copious amounts of beer and scotch.

Two days before our departure, Franck developed a dental abscess and I came down with a bronchial infection. Instead of careening around the Royal Mile we stayed in our postage stamp sized apartment in the *rue des Fossés Saint Bernard* just behind Notre Dame. That night, cuddled on our hand-me-down mattress we watched our grainy black and white television that was about the size of a Kleenex box and captured channels with a radio dial. Franck, who had undergone half a root canal the day before and had to withstand the second half in two days' time, propped the TV on his stomach. I made us each a bowl of *Blédina* – a vegetable puree that all French babies adore – and that was about the only thing Franck could get down. And we ate our baby food while we watched some obscure movie about a girl who goes back in time to the Middle Ages. We were both unconscious by the time one year ceded to the next.

The next day we woke early, medicated ourselves heavily, wound long scarves around our necks, and wandered through the empty streets of our *quartier*, holding hands. I had never seen the streets of Paris so quiet or the cafés so deserted. We stole into a modest café on the Boulevard Saint Germain with a long zinc counter. On top was a metal rack of hard-boiled eggs for sale. We bought one each, and ordered strong black espressos to wash them down.

Franck leaned over the zinc and kissed my lips, still salty from my egg.

"I think this is the best New Year's I've ever had," he said. I kissed him again in agreement.

Why then did I make a habit of trying to wrestle the universe into submission, forcing it to deliver joy and happiness on demand? It was silly, I realized as I sipped my *Corton* and watched the Crazy Horse girls strut. Joy always snuck up on us when it was least expected.

The week after our restful Crazy Horse New Year's celebration, Franck called Olivier several times to ask if he'd heard from Gégé. We idly wondered if he'd been kidnapped by aliens or merely forgotten all about his promise to visit us.

"Should I call him?" Franck mused when we bumped into Olivier a week later at the *boulangerie* across from Franck's house.

"I wouldn't," Olivier said. "Be patient."

Patience. That was something we did not have. The only thing we felt equipped to do was scrape off old wallpaper, and we were getting close to the end of that with only the kitchen and the living room left to go. We only had three months and three weeks left before our first guests arrived. Olivier was asking the impossible.

Five long and impatient days later, I heard an unfamiliar scratching sound while I was scraping in the living room. I whipped around just in time to see a waft of smoke curl around the front door which I had left open a crack in an attempt to chase away the rubber smell. I lunged across the entrance tiles and flung the door open.

Gégé stood there, eyebrow cocked. "Waiting for someone?"

I was far past playing it cool. "*Oui*! You!" I grabbed the sleeve of his green utility jacket and dragged him inside, then shut the door firmly behind him.

I gave him a hearty *bises* on each cheek. "*Un café?*" He nodded, slightly stunned and let me push him into the kitchen.

The phone rang and I heard Franck pick it up in the bedroom. "Franck!" I hollered, not wanting to leave Gégé's side in case he tried to sneak away. "Gégé's here! We'll be in the kitchen having a *café*."

One of my very best Christmas gifts that year was a cornflower blue coffee maker given to me by Stéphanie. Coloured household appliances were one of the things I loved about France. Who, after all, declared that coffee makers and toasters and kettles should only be white, black or beige?

By the time Franck joined us the coffee was made and Gégé and I were enjoying a second cup each. Gégé didn't say much but I talked enough for both of us, rattling on just to keep him nailed to his chair by the centrifugal force of my verbal diarrhoea.

The two of them shook hands and Franck leaned over and gave me a kiss that I knew was thanks for being wily enough to trap our potential saviour in the kitchen.

"Bonjour Gégé. I see Laura's been looking after you."

Gégé blushed right up to the bald spot on the crown of his head. Franck served himself a coffee while Gégé recovered his nonchalance. His attention became riveted by the underside of the staircase leading up to the attic.

"I've never seen such a crooked staircase," he said finally. "The stonemason who built it must have been completely sloshed."

"Maybe we could knock it out and put - " Franck began.

"*Non!*" I said. "I like that it's crooked." Franck and Gégé both looked at me. "It gives the house character," I explained.

"We could have a much bigger kitchen," Franck reminded me.

I shrugged. "I don't care."

Gégé raised one thin brow. "Franck told me Canadians were strange about old things. To think I didn't believe him."

"You see?" Franck raked back the black hair out of his eyes.

"Anyway," Gégé concluded, "I'm not sure you could take down the staircase without the house falling around your ears. That's the way these old stone houses were built." He tapped his fingers on the tabletop. "Want to show me the rest of this castle of yours?"

We started the grand tour in the bedroom that overlooked the church.

"*Bon Dieu*." Gégé placed a hand on the slanting wall. "These walls must have been laid by the same stonemason." He made a circle with his thumb and forefinger and twisted it around his nose – the French symbol for drunk. He meandered over to the window which boasted beautiful, albeit rusty, metal fixtures with an ornate handle.

"Single pane," he sighed. "No wonder it's freezing in here. Not to mention *that*." He pointed up to the large patch of plaster on the ceiling above the window that was falling down in flaking yellow chunks. "And *that!*" He waved at the hole I had made in the wall. "*L'humidité.*" Humidity. He imbued this word with the same death-knoll tone as Franck.

"So…you'll need new windows…" Gégé began. Franck extracted the notebook he carried in the worn back pocket of his jeans and started scribbling. "I can do electricity and plumbing but not plaster, tiling, or windows," Gégé informed us. "For those things, we'll need to find somebody else."

Franck frowned, and scribbled something else down. I inwardly rejoiced at Gégé's use of "we" as though it went without saying that he was already part of our team. I tried not to smile though. I sensed that if anything could scare Gégé away from our disaster it would be boisterous enthusiasm.

"Nice floors." Gégé turned his attention to the oak parquet underneath our feet. He kneeled down and laid his hand on them. "These rooms are over the passageway, *hein*? Feel this floor. It's freezing." Franck gave an apologetic shrug in the affirmative.

Gégé beckoned us down to his level, and we both placed reluctant hands on the beautifully worn and old floorboards. The glacial air coming up from between the strips of oak took my breath away.

"There's probably no insulation between the floorboards and the plaster on the top of the passageway. It's a wind tunnel down there." More problems and we hadn't even made it to the second bedroom. Suddenly the renovation budget that we had planned of 50,000 francs seemed like a pittance. A knot formed under my sternum.

The visit continued in much the same vein as we revisited the kitchen (bad plumbing and no space for a dishwasher, not to mention the parlous state of the single paned window), the living room (the tile floor near the fireplace was irretrievably stained, and the fireplace could probably never be used again), and the WC (linked up to a septic tank, meaning no end to the problems that entailed), until we reached the end of the line, the bathroom with its turquoise fittings and meager hot water.

Gégé climbed up onto the rim of the bathtub to inspect a patch of the wall where there was a big dark splotch on the wallpaper.

"Do you have a hammer?" he asked Franck.

By the time Franck brought it to him Gégé had peeled off the wallpaper that was barely clinging to the wall, revealing a sprawling orange stain underneath. He began to hit the wall with the hammer as Franck and I watched. Franck reached for my hand, his eyes filled with foreboding. A shower of plaster rained down with each hit. The hole got deeper and deeper. Would he end up in the neighbour's living room? Oh well, I reasoned, seeing as we hadn't been graced with a visit from the *cadastre* yet the neighbor still owned our bathroom anyway. Still, maybe this wasn't the best time for us to burst through his wall.

The chunks of plaster that fell from the hole got bigger and bigger, but instead of looking grimmer Gégé's shy smile grew. At last the hammer clunked on something more solid sounding than the muffled 'shlunk' of wet plaster.

"*Le voilà!*" He beckoned us over with a crooked finger.

The hole in our wall was about half a foot deep. Franck and I peered inside, neither of us particularly enthusiastic about the prospect of what we were going to see.

"*La pierre!*" Gégé crowed as I took in the sight of Burgundy's famous pink and ochre stone covered by a fine layer of white dust.

I didn't know what to think. I'd always wanted exposed stone walls, or *pierres apparentes* as the French called them, but I'd also heard that they took an epic amount of work — not to mention a stonemason - to uncover and restore properly.

"Is that good or bad?" Franck asked, cautious.

"It's certainly not good!" Gégé exclaimed with joy.

"I've always wanted a wall in *pierres apparentes*," I said. "Does this mean…"

Gégé snorted with laughter and jumped down to the irretrievably-stained tile floor. "*Impossible*. There's plumbing and wiring running through the plaster."

"So what can we do then?" Franck asked.

Gégé took a last appreciative glance into the hole. "Dig out these rotten spots, refill, and re-plaster." He lit a cigarette with a langor that I normally associated with post-coitus. "Are you religious?"

Franck glanced at me. Not *this* conversation again. I shrugged. "Sort of. Sometimes. Depends."

"In that case" - Gégé let out a short, staccato of a laugh - "I would recommend a lot of prayer."

Thirty minutes later Gégé was back at the kitchen table, cheerfully outlining his plan for digging out the humid sections of the walls and re-plastering them. The only problem was, he seemed delighted to remind us, that plastering, like the making of a truly good baguette, required un *sacré coup de main*, or skill, which he simply did not possess.

"I can learn," Franck said. "But I need somebody to teach me."

Gégé played with his cigarette for a very long time. "I may have an idea," he said, just when I began to worry that he had gone mute. "Paulo."

"'Paulo?" I echoed. Was this a place or a thing or a person?

"A friend of mine from work. He talks non-stop, but if you can put up with that there's no better plasterer."

"What's his number?" Franck asked.

"He's Portuguese," Gégé added, a stickler for full disclosure.

"So?" I asked.

"Hot-blooded. Good guy, but never disagree with him or interrupt him when he's telling a story. I'm warning you, he tells a *lot* of stories."

"Can he talk and plaster at the same time?" Franck said.

Gégé considered this and then blew a puff of air between his lips. "*Pourquoi pas?*"

Franck nodded. "Let's call him."

CHAPTER 19

From that day on, Gégé arrived in the morning with a hearty appetite for disaster and a bag of hot croissants and *pains au chocolat* from his favourite baker in Nuits-Saint-Georges. By the end of the first day I knew he took his coffee piping hot and with three sugars. Gégé had a call in to his friend Paulo, the Portuguese plasterer, but the word was he had gone to Portugal and no one seemed entirely sure when he'd be back. Franck, Gégé, and I surmised that maybe he was having a stolen vacation with the *cadastre*, or surveyor, who had cancelled two visits to our house and now managed to be "out of the office" every time we called.

"At least we still have the furniture," Franck said. "I'm starting to hope that the owners' children have forgotten all about it."

I knocked on the wooden table top for luck. They had said they would call us after Christmas to set up a time to pick up everything, but it was now mid-January and we hadn't heard a peep out of them. I wasn't sure what we would do if they did in fact remember. If we did only what Gégé insisted was the bare minimum needed for our reno, we would have absolutely no money left over to buy ourselves so much as a solitary chair.

A few days after Gégé became part of our team the three of us finally scraped off the last bit of wallpaper. Franck frowned at the yellowish stained plaster underneath.

"What can we do next without Paulo? We can't afford to waste any time."

"I can help you dig out the wet plaster," Gégé offered. "We should do that first before we re-plumb the bathroom and the kitchen."

They started in the living room and made huge cavernous holes in the plaster. I grew used to the 'thunk' of pick axes and the 'shlunk' of wet plaster falling to the ground. I poured over paint chips and plotted out the paint colors we would use once the now hideous walls were made pristine.

I was contemplating a marvellous shade of poppy when the phone rang. I heard Franck pick it up and from his hesitation and then formal use of "*vous*", I knew it wasn't any of his family or friends. I hurried into the living room and tried not to notice the swiftly multiplying craters in the walls.

"Is it *le cadastre*?" I mouthed to Franck, bouncing on my toes.

Franck's lips pressed into a thin line and he shook his head. "Tonight?" he said in the speaker. "Yes, that would be just fine. How about seven?" He nodded and then hung up the phone.

"*Alors?* Who was it?"

"It was for the furniture." Franck tossed his pick-axe down with a clatter. "The seller's children didn't forget. They've just been busy. They'll be coming by tonight to arrange the move."

I slumped down on a chair. "*Zut.*"

Gégé had come back up from the cellar where he had dumped off another load of wet plaster. His brown eyes shifted from Franck to me and back again.

"Does this mean you already know about the snakes?" he demanded.

Snakes?" Franck and I both echoed.

"In the cellar." Gégé gingerly lifted up Franck's pick-axe from the table and transferred it to the chimney ledge on the far side of the room. "A nest of them."

"What kind of snakes?" Franck asked, quietly and almost menacingly. I knew how he felt. Gégé was only the messenger, but I simply felt like I couldn't take one more shred of bad news.

"*Les couleuvres*," Gégé said. "At least they're not poisonous like vipers. But if you didn't know about them, why do you both look like you've just smelled an *Époisses* cheese?"

That got a smile out of me. Even Franck's lips twitched. "That was one of the children of the previous owner on the phone. They're coming tonight to arrange picking up all our furniture."

"Their furniture," Gégé noted.

Franck and I glowered at him. He laughed. "That is a problem, but not one you can do much about. You should have negotiated to buy all the furniture when you bought the house."

Gégé had a gift for giving sterling advice when it was far too late to act upon it.

"Well, we didn't," Franck said. "Where exactly are the snakes anyway?"

"I didn't get close enough to count and just for the record I won't be going down to the cellar unless you do something about them. I am terrified of snakes." Rather than being embarrassed about what many people would consider a weakness, Gégé straightened his shoulders and lifted his chin in pride at this fact.

"I'll go down to the cellar." Franck's eyes were dancing now. "I imagine I can get rid of the nest too, although I've never actually done that before."

"Olivier got rid of one last year," Gégé said. "We should go to him for advice."

I checked the time. It was five o'clock. "OK, but we have to be back here by seven."

"Perfect." Gégé shrugged on his camouflage jacket. "We'll just be in time for *l'apéritif*."

Olivier welcomed us warmly. Within five minutes of being ushered through his doorway I was happily ensconced in front of the fire sipping a *kir*, almost grateful to the snakes. I needed a bit of a respite before our furniture was whisked away from underneath us. I listened with only half an ear to the conversation between the three men.

"They looked big," Gégé was insisting with regard to the new denizens of our cellar.

Olivier guffawed. "I'm sure they were only the babies. The parents like to hide their nests in the pipes."

Gégé blanched.

"I'll get them out for you if you find any when you're doing the plumbing."

"Your hands are too big. Laura will have to do it."

I snapped to attention. "Excuse me?"

Olivier looked shocked, as though he had forgotten I was there, and leapt up to freshen my drink which to my surprise I had almost finished already. "Chances are you won't find any in the pipes, Laura. Gégé surely scared them away with his little girl screams."

Gégé brushed a cobweb off his work jumper. "They took me by surprise."

I smiled. "Don't forget to tell us when it's six thirty," I reminded Olivier, and took a few more sips of my *kir*. Fat flakes of snow had begun to drift past Olivier's window. I shut my eyes for just a moment.

I was woken by Franck shaking me.

"We're late!" he grasped me under the armpits and pulled me up. "Why weren't you watching the time? You *always* watch the time."

"I asked Olivier..." I began, but then caught sight of several empty bottles on the table and the well-used tarot cards hastily laid down. Franck was swaying; he held me as though we were waltzing. Olivier blinked mistily at me.

"You're all drunk!"

Gégé attempted to stand up, then collapsed on his chair again. "That may be why my legs won't work."

"What time is it anyway?"

Gégé peered down at his watch. "Twenty to eight."

Franck swore explosively and dragged me out of the house.

I shivered in the cold. The snow was still coming down in fat clumps and it was impossible to make out where the road had been.

"Our car can't drive in this," Franck stated the obvious.

"As if you should be driving anyway!" I said. Just then Dominique's car crept along the snow towards us and the window opened.

Franck waved at her. "How are the roads?" he asked.

"What roads?" she said. "You can't see them anymore."

"Can we get a drive to Magny?" Franck asked. "We're really late and - "

"Get in!" She waved towards the back seat. "It's getting worse by the second."

"Maybe they're late too," I surmised, looking out at the white drifts outside the car window.

"Come to think of it, I'm sure they didn't even set out at all," Franck hiccuped. "I mean, look at it out there!" He began to nuzzle my neck in the back seat while I prayed – to the Virgin Mary, Jesus, God, Franck's guardian angels or anyone else who would listen - that the seller's children had decided not to come.

Dominique dropped us off in front of the church and I half dragged, half pushed my very merry husband under the stone archway of our house. A car with fogged up windows and several people inside was parked at the bottom of our steps. Judging from the thick layer of snow on the car roof they had been waiting for us for quite some time already. This time anyway, my prayers hadn't been answered.

Our arriving over an hour late was not a propitious start to the negotiations. I had been hoping to sweet talk them into selling us the pieces of furniture I loved - like the kitchen buffet, the pine table, the rosewood bedside table with the marble top - for a cheap price.

"They're going to be furious." I peered through the driving snow as we trudged towards their car.

"I forgot to tell you," Franck said, his voice pregnant with humor. "We will probably need their attestation when we are finally able to meet with the surveyor."

"Attesting to what?"

"That our neighbour doesn't own half of our house." I could make out some pinched faces inside the steamed-up car now.

"I can't believe you drank so much," I began. "I can't believe you didn't - "

"Let's divide and conquer." Franck shut me up with a kiss, dropped the clutch of keys in my hand and pushed me towards the stairs. "Remember what Réné said about not confusing what is urgent with what is truly important. Go and open the door and turn on the lights."

I took the snowy stairs two at a time, unlocked the doors in record time and turned on every light switch within reach. Before I knew it, Franck had ushered our visitors, three men and a tall, angular woman, out of their car and was jollying them up the stairs. In the front hall he divested them of their jackets and scarves before they could so much as utter a protest. He apologized charmingly for our *retard* and explained that we had been discussing with our plumber the best way to remove snakes from pipes over a few *kir*.

The shortest man sniffed. "We were just about to leave."

Franck tutted at this and shepherded them into the living room. "That would have been a shame as I wouldn't have had the pleasure of offering you a drink. *Kir?*" He found chairs for everyone and beckoned them to take a seat.

Franck's Burgundian charm, even turned up to full wattage, slid off our guests like eggs on Teflon. They sat silently and surveyed the room with pained expressions. I followed their eyes. Ah yes, the holes in the wall. Preoccupied with the snakes in our cellar, I had momentarily forgotten about those.

The tallest man nodded curtly. "*Kir* would be fine but we will not be staying long."

"The weather is dreadful," Franck agreed, but the man stared at him as if to drive home the point that the weather was not the reason for their speedy departure.

Franck waved me to the table. "Laura, you sit down with our guests. I'll get the glasses."

I cursed Franck under my breath but took my seat. The silence around the table was full of reproach. I meticulously arranged my jacket across the back of my chair.

"I'm so sorry for the wait," I said, finally. "We have at last found someone to help us with the renovations and so we have to go where he wants us to go. There is just so much to do here."

The shortest man, who also sported an impressively florid nose, sniffed around the room. "What needs renovating? This house is" - his lips curled back as he surveyed the pock-marked walls - "or rather, *was* in pristine condition."

I followed his affronted gaze around the peeling flower-explosion wallpaper and the cracked plaster of the ceiling.

"I guess *renovations* isn't the right word." I made an apologetic gesture with my hand. "My French, you know…"

Franck swept into the room carrying a tray laden with bottles and six glasses. I was impressed despite myself that he could do it so steadily with all that *cassis* and white wine flowing through his veins. "A bit of freshening up, *c'est tout!*" he finished for me.

The woman, a sinewy, nervous sort, began to blink furiously. Her eyes became shiny and worked their way over every inch of the room. "I so loved coming here. We'd wake up in the morning to the sound of the bells and then have our bowls of chicory in the kitchen. The house still has the same smell."

Mothballs and burning rubber? I wanted to ask.

"I love the bells too," I said, instead. "Whenever I wake up in the middle of the night or in the early morning I can tell what time it is without ever having to look at the clock. They don't have church bells like that in Canada."

They all turned to me, interested despite themselves. "*Vraiment?* No bells? What is on the churches then?"

"It's true." Franck picked up the gauntlet and in an amazing feat of multi-tasking, proceeded to pour them drinks and pass them out while regaling them with the confounding state of religion in Canada, where even "cults" — as the French considered Jehovah's Witnesses and Scientologists — could have their church anywhere they pleased – even beside a real (meaning Catholic) church. There was much marveling over this, and several times I was called upon to confirm that Franck wasn't merely pulling their leg.

"If you have never been to North America, especially the West Coast, I think it is difficult for you to understand how very new everything is," I said. "That's why I love your mother's house so much."

The shortest man looked like he was near tears now. "My mother lived here during the war, you know. My father was a prisoner in Germany for two years. There are probably letters from him up in the attic. A German soldier had to be billeted here with us. Of course, he took the best bedroom, the one that looks out onto the church. She put up with him though. She put up with so much, and now to think…"

Two large, round tears rolled down his cheeks. His sister reached across the table and grabbed his hand. "We didn't have any choice," she said in a faint voice.

"She never wanted to leave this house! She always said so!"

"She couldn't take care of herself anymore," the sister's husband intervened, sounding exasperated. "It was becoming dangerous. She was going to burn the whole village down with those damn cigarillos of hers."

"It must have been a very difficult decision for you to make," I said.

"It's not like they threw her out in the street!" The husband rolled his eyes. "She's in a lovely retirement home in the South. I can only dream that my children will pay for *me* to go and live in Uzès! I would eat olives and drink *Pastis* all day long. Trust me – your mother is surely doing exactly the same and not weeping and wailing over her sort. She's far from stupid, although she is gifted at riddling her children with guilt."

The taller brother waved away the brewing argument. "We need to figure out who wants what. I want these chairs." He pointed at the coloured cane chairs that he was perched upon and then looked around the room. "Not much else."

"They go nicely with the buffet." I gestured up to the object of my nightmares.

"*Oui*, I suppose they do." My heart rose with hope. "*Maman* always loved that buffet. She would spend hours polishing it. My ceilings, *hélas*, are just too low. It is very valuable, I'm sure, but someone else will have to take it." He rubbed his chin as his eyes travelled up the expanse of dark wood. "It goes perfectly in this room. It would be a shame to move it anywhere else."

"I agree," the woman said. "It would never fit in my little house. Besides, Patrice has a bad back." Her husband made a show of reaching back and rubbing his spine with a grimace. I didn't miss, however, the relief in his eyes.

The shortest brother stood up and ran a delicate finger down the fat barleycorn corkscrews of wood. "Do you remember mother polishing this? She always said it was the kind of furniture that was made for aristocrats. She said it made her feel like a *duchesse*."

"You want it?" his older brother asked.

"Of course…"

"Franck could help you move it," I jumped in, avoiding Franck's eyes. "His back is exceptionally strong."

"Of course I would take it if I could," the short brother continued, "but it might frighten my cat. Robert is right. It goes so well in this room. It belongs here."

The four of them smiled benevolently at Franck and me. A hook of guilt caught inside my chest. I cleared my throat and tried to ignore the weight of Franck's foot coming down on mine. What I was about to say went against all of Franck's deeply held Burgundian precepts of gratitude and hospitality, but I had to say it nonetheless.

"I don't like the buffet." Four sets of eyes widened in amazement. Franck's were telegraphing me desperately to backtrack while I still could. "I don't think I would keep it, even if you left it here. I would probably sell it to a *brocante*."

"*Mais...pourquoi?*" The woman demanded, getting teary again. "It is so very *élégante*."

They waited for my answer. Franck took advantage to do the only thing that was left for him to do now that I had desecrated the *ambiance*. He poured everyone another *kir*.

I shrugged. "I suppose one can't explain tastes."

"*Non*," agreed the eldest brother, eyeing me with patent dislike.

"I really think one of you should take it," I insisted.

This was followed by a babble of protests. As much as they all professed their undying love for the buffet, none of them seemed to carry that love so far as to welcome the monstrosity into their own abode.

Franck cast me a dirty look as he finished pouring the *kir*. "I won't lie to you," he said, to them. "We do need some furniture to get started. We don't really have anything of our own, not even a bed."

"Not even a bed!" the woman exclaimed to Franck, ignoring me. "*Mais alors*! We cannot take your bed!"

With this the eldest brother hauled himself up to his feet. "I suppose we should look around at what's here. Where should we start?"

Franck led all of us into the far bedroom – the one with the window that looked onto the church and the neighbors' boisterous roosters and ever-pecking chickens – the bedroom that the German soldier had picked out for himself.

The beds in here had been removed. All that remained was the prim little wooden bedside table with a marble top. "One bedside table." The eldest brother scribbled down on a pad of paper he had extracted from somewhere.

The inner bedroom was next, the one that led out onto the veranda. There was an old bed frame here, with a rose carved in the wood but no mattress on the bed.

"My mother insisted on taking that mattress to Uzès with her," the younger brother explained, apologetic. "It must have dated back to the war, perhaps even the first one. I know for a fact it was stuffed with dusty old horsehairs. She insisted she could sleep on nothing else."

Then we continued into the kitchen, which was furnished with a rudimentary oven and fridge, as well as the battered kitchen table that I quite adored, and the charming kitchen buffet. It had been varnished with some horrendous faux-wood sticky stuff but I was sure clear pine was underneath. Contrary to the beast in the living room, I had loved the kitchen buffet from the moment I set eyes on it. I held my breath. It was a far easier piece of furniture to move than the living room buffet. Which one of them would claim it?

"We don't have anywhere to store dishes except this buffet,' Franck said, feigning an offhand tone. "If you want it, go ahead and take it, but if you don't want it maybe we could buy it from you."

The brothers, sister, and brother-in-law didn't answer. They all appeared to be busy thinking. We quickly toured the other rooms, where Franck pointed out the few items that we were interested in buying from them, including the sofa bed. We finished back in the living room.

"I think I could use that kitchen buffet in my garage," mused the youngest brother, taking a deep pull on his *kir*. "It would be handy for storing my tools." I suppressed a shudder. Everyone had sat down again, everyone but Franck.

"We're not done yet," he announced, a gleam in his eye. "We've forgotten the attic."

Four pairs of eyes widened in horror.

"Come on." Franck waved them up. "We must discuss how you are going to go about sorting through all the treasures up there. "

The attic was absolutely packed with towering boxes of papers and old cast iron pans and what looked like little glass jars that Franck had told me were "*les ventouses*", which used to be steamed up then vacuum-sucked onto the back of anyone suffering from ailments ranging from impotence to lumbago. Apparently Franck's *Pépé Georges* swore by

160

them. It was amazing that the rotting floorboards in the attic didn't collapse under the weight of over a century's worth of accumulated stuff.

Franck dug out a flashlight from the drawer of the buffet.

"Laura, while we are up there can you go and fetch a fresh bottle of *crémant* from the cellar?" He winked at me as he passed by. What was he up to? In any case, the attic always gave me an asthma attack and I vastly preferred snakes to a trip to the ER.

Our guests' shoulders slumped as they grudgingly began to make their way up the crooked stairs behind Franck. By the time I returned from the cellar the attic stairs were disgorging them one by one. They were all coughing and brushing dust off their shoulders. Franck brought up the rear with an almost undetectable upturn of his lips.

"I'm sure you cannot wait to go through all of those boxes!" I exclaimed to the younger brother. He slumped back in his chair and picked a dusty cobweb off the sleeve of his fine lamb's wool sweater. Franck gave me an infinitesimal nod of encouragement before ducking into the kitchen.

"I don't think there's much of value," the younger brother muttered.

"Maybe not monetary value," I said. "But as for sentimental value…it will be like a treasure hunt. How exciting!"

"I'm not sorting through that *bordel*," his sister announced to her brothers. "Don't think you will make me do it because I'm the only female. I refuse."

Her husband ducked under the doorway, his head festooned with a few very mouldy pieces of straw. "It smells like rat poison up there. Your *maman* must have doused everything in it."

The elder brother followed. "She did. I'd forgotten how she loved her rat poison."

"Rat poison?" I echoed.

The elder man waved away my worried look. "Doesn't kill people. At least…I don't think it does."

Franck came in just then with another bottle of *cassis* and the fresh bottle of *crémant* I had retrieved from the cellar. One dark, rueful eyebrow was raised.

"I don't envy you the job," he sighed as he poured everyone fresh and very generous drinks. He crooked his finger at me when he was done. "Laura and I will just go into the kitchen to cut up some *saucisson sec.*"

We scuttled to the kitchen. I passed Franck a *saucisson* out of the fridge and watched as he skillfully, but far more slowly than usual, peeled away its thin skin and cut it up into delicate, paper thin slices.

The murmur of voices in urgent consultation came through the wall.

"What do you - " I began, but Franck shushed me with a *cassis*-laced kiss.

Finally the murmurs began to die down. I spread out the *saucisson* slices on a small wooden cutting board. Franck armed himself with a basket of freshly cut bread and we shared a smile before gliding back into the living room. Franck topped up everyone's glasses and I passed the *saucisson* around to the general praise of all.

"So," Franck began. "When would you like to come and pick up the furniture? I imagine you can take some of the smaller things today and get started with some of the boxes from the attic, but I suppose you'll need to rent a small truck for the bigger items."

On the other side of the table all eyes went to the tallest brother. He lifted his glass. "Actually, we are not sure that...well...how much would you pay us for it?"

"For what *exactement?*" Franck asked.

The man swept his hand around the room. "Everything."

"Everything?" I asked.

"Except these chairs, *bien sûr.*" He wrapped a hand around the wooden leg of the chair he sat upon. "I still want these."

Franck delicately inserted a *saucisson* in his mouth and took his time chewing. All eyes were riveted on him but I spoke first.

"To tell you the truth, after buying the house and with the reno...I mean, the re-decorating we have planned, we really don't have much money." I wasn't trying to be some kind of brilliant negotiator. In fact, that had been one of my big problems in law school - I would always just blurt out the truth.

"We could use the fridge and the stove," Franck reminded me. "We'd have to go out and buy those anyway."

"And the kitchen buffet," I added.

"But we want to leave it all!" The smaller man slapped his palm on the table to underline his point.

"Except my chairs," his brother reminded him.

Silence descended on the table. We chewed on our *saucisson*, eyes darting from one to another.

"The fact of the matter is that none of us have the *courage* to clear out the attic," the sister explained at last. Her husband and brothers nodded in enthusiastic agreement. "So if we can agree on a price it would be for everything – except these chairs. It would mean we wouldn't have to come back and get any of it."

Franck considered this. "That's going to be a lot of work for us, going through the attic. I don't know if we have the time."

The elder brother cracked his knuckles. "We understand that, but to compensate for your troubles we would give you a deal on the rest."

"Did you have a number in mind?" Franck's eyes gleamed. He loved negotiating. Not so much for the cheaper price, but for the sheer sport of the activity. He had visited Tunisia with his aunt and uncle when he was a teenager and wiled away many afternoons sipping mint tea at the *souk* while watching the lively negotiations bounce back and forth over the rugs.

The elder brother fingered the stem of his wine glass and met the eye of his brother and sister, who both gave him infinitesimal nods. "Twenty thousand for all of it."

"We don't have twenty thousand!" I burst out, and under the table Franck's foot trod again on mine.

"Fifteen then," the sister said quickly.

"Ten thousand," Franck said. "That's all we could possibly pay, and even that would be a stretch for us. We'll give you a moment to chat."

I picked up the now empty cutting board and followed Franck into the kitchen. He pulled me close.

"Good negotiating," he whispered in my ear. "It'll work. You should have seen their expressions when they saw the *bordel* in the attic."

The murmured, urgent voices from the other side of the wall died down once again and we walked back into the living room together. The elder brother slowly pushed his chair back and put out his hand.

"You've got a deal, but I'm taking these chairs with me today."

CHAPTER 20

It was the beginning of February and things seemed to be turning our way. Paulo was back from Portugal and due to call on us in a few days' time. We had been able to keep all the furniture and even found a few spare rickety wooden chairs in the attic to replace the ones that were taken. The baby snakes in the cellar had apparently been frightened away, as Olivier had surmised, by Gégé's shrieking, and Franck and Gégé had only the two bedrooms left to eviscerate before Paulo could show them how to patch up the walls again with plaster.

Even more phenomenal was that Franck had managed to talk to the surveyor on the phone that morning, finally convincing him to pay us a visit to discuss the zoning dilemma at two o'clock.

At one thirty, after a quick lunch of green salad and leek and goat cheese quiches bought from the *boulangerie,* Franck pushed himself back from the table.

"What time is it?"

Gégé burped softly and consulted his watch. "One thirty."

"We should go and wait outside for him."

"He's not due for another half hour," I said. "It's not like you to be early for anything."

"He'll take any opportunity to leave again," Franck said. "We'll have to lie in wait and leap out in front of his car if necessary." Now that Gégé had finished his lunch with us, part of me expected him to beat a hasty retreat and let Franck and me deal with the elusive civil servant. Instead he followed us outside, lit yet another cigarette and leaned against the wall of the passageway, waiting for the curtain to go up on the next act of the Laura-and-Franck-and-their-falling-apart-half-owned-house show.

The wind howled underneath the passageway where we huddled in the cold. I leaned into the blessed comfort of Franck's ski jacket. His warmth and faint scent of apples flowed through me and my thoughts drifted back to an Open House day at one of the top solicitors' firms in London.

Oxford shepherded its final year law students around all of the City's legal institutions. We had a choice to make – become a barrister or become a solicitor. One had to be either ridiculously brilliant or brilliantly well connected in order to become a barrister, so the huge majority of us had reconciled ourselves to becoming solicitors. After months of wearing jeans and wool sweaters to my tutorials I wrestled myself into a pair of pantyhose and heels. That in itself was enough to make me feel resentful toward the officious trainee solicitor who had been assigned to show me around the firm.

"Do you have a boyfriend?" she asked me. I scurried to keep up with her as her chic pumps stalked down the carpeted hallway from the corporate to the litigation department.

"Yes, actually…"

"You won't for long," she shot back.

"Actually, I have a husband. We got married last summer."

She paused with her hand on the handle of a heavy oak door. "It makes no difference. You'll end up divorced by the time you finish your articling. I guarantee it."

I could not hide my scepticism.

"You don't believe me?" she cross-examined. "Just how do you plan to maintain a relationship with anyone outside of work if you never see them?"

"There's always the weekend."

"You'll be working."

"Evenings?"

"You'll be working."

"Not *every* - "I began.

"I sleep here at least twice a week. Usually more."

"So you don't have a boyfriend?"

"I do." Her sharp features rearranged themselves in a smug

expression. "He works here. It's the only way."

With that she swept me into a buzzing department of lawyers who seemed to live on a strict regimen of coffee and contention. The youngest ones – the articling students – could be identified by their pallor and the black circles under their eyes.

I tried to convince myself that my guide was spouting nonsense; Franck and I were stronger than she could possibly know. As the tour wore on, however, I chatted with more trainees and freshly qualified legal eagles: a fleshy cheeked guy probably younger than me who was already working on the prodigious beginnings of a beer belly, a nattily dressed East Indian woman, and a dandy in a pin-striped suit and pink tie. They all confirmed what she had said. Affairs between colleagues were rampant. Spouses and significant others had a way of drifting away due to sheer neglect.

"Is it worth it?" I asked the dandy with an earnestness that seemed to give him pause. "Do you actually like your work?"

He tugged on one pinstriped lapel. "To be perfectly honest, I loathe my job but I'm sticking at it for the same reason as everyone else around here does."

"Which is?"

"Money, of course. Once you make partner, you've got it made."

Franck's arms tightened around me now, but despite my jacket and his warmth I began to shiver.

"Go back inside," Franck said to me. "There's no point in us all freezing out here."

We had already been waiting ten minutes and, without saying a word, Gégé had proved his theory about the passageway being a formidable wind tunnel. I consoled myself with the fact that the wind chill factor probably diminished any satisfaction he felt about this fact. Just then Gégé leapt out into the icy road and in front of a slowly crawling white *camionette*.

"It's him! I'm sure of it!"

I blinked. Gégé was ready to risk life and limb for our cause. Employing the same imperiousness with which he had chastised Olivier for his sub-floor, he waved the *camionette* over towards the parking spots in front of the church.

The driver of the *camionette* wore a distinctly cornered look on his middle-aged face. I hadn't really believed it when Franck and Gégé

167

swore that the *cadastre* would use any excuse to drive off, but it looked like they were right.

The *cadastre* had rearranged his features in an expression of strained civility by the time he wrapped his scarf around his neck and unfolded his lanky body out of the car.

"*Bonjour*," he said and regretfully shook all of our icy hands.

"Let's go inside." Franck ushered everyone back into the house again. Once inside, the *cadastre* extracted a roll of drawing paper from his jacket and unrolled it on the kitchen table. He didn't take his jacket off. Clearly he did not plan to bestow much of his sacred time on us. His preamble came in the form of a majestic sigh.

"You have a problem," he said. "According to this, your neighbour owns more than half of your house."

Franck's smoking finger twitched. "We know. How could this happen? How could this mistake be carried on when it is clearly not a reflection of the actual division between the houses?"

The surveyor cleaned his glasses on his scarf and let a puff of air escape between his lips. "It happens. Either nobody has noticed or, if they have, nobody has cared enough to do anything. Maybe they just figured there was an understanding between neighbours."

"So it's easy to resolve?" Franck asked.

"That all depends on your neighbour." The *cadastre* cocked an eyebrow.

Gégé, who was familiar with the neighbour in question, snorted.

Franck's mouth tightened. "I haven't had any problems with him so far, but he has a...certain reputation. According to the other neighbors, he is quite intent on acquiring more property around his house."

"Isn't he in for a nice surprise!" The surveyor laughed. Franck lost no time in giving him an "*oeil noir*" which quickly snuffed the hilarity. The *cadastre* smoothed out his plans.

"You need to talk to your neighbor about this. That is where you must start."

"I did quite some time ago, but we weren't able to conclude anything. Maybe with you here- "

"*Attendez!*" The *cadastre* stood up, his face pink with alarm. "I meant *after* I leave."

"I'll go get him right now." Franck was quickly out the door. Le *cadastre* looked at me accusingly.

"This is highly irregular. You know I am a busy man. I am already late for another meeting."

"He won't be long," I assured him. "Our neighbour probably isn't even home anyway."

The surveyor looked as though he was about to leave. Gégé was blocking the doorway, but he was much smaller than the *cadastre*.

"I don't quite understand where the two houses are separated. Can you show me on the plans again?" I stalled.

He had just begun tracing the outline of our house on the plans with his finger when a heavily accented voice overpowered the bell across the street chiming three o'clock.

"*Bah*! It makes no sense!" Monsieur De Luca bellowed as he strode into our kitchen, Franck in his wake. His massive shoulders and red face seemed to suck the air from the room. His fists, clenched to his sides, were like two medium-sized cabbages. Even the *cadastre*, who had stood up to shake the neighbor's hand and introduce himself, didn't dare make any attempts to leave now.

"Would you like a coffee?" I asked. Monsieur De Luca turned to me with wide eyes as though seeing me for the first time. "Please sit down," I ushered him to chair, making the most of the fact that he seemed unnerved to find a woman in the midst of all of this. "Do you take sugar?"

Franck slipped into the third chair and indicated to the dazed *cadastre* that he could begin with the explanations.

"It would appear as though, according to our plans, you own two thirds of Monsieur and Madame Germain's house."

The idiot! There were a hundred better ways to present the problem.

The *cadastre* pushed the set of plans under Monsieur De Luca's nose and, shrinking away slightly, traced his finger over the red line that showed the separation of our two houses. Everyone except Monsieur De Luca held their breath. Our neighbor traced the line on the plan with a finger roughly the same diameter as a *saucisson sec*.

"How can this be?" he said, finally. "My house is my house." He waved a fist at Franck. "His house is his house."

I suppressed a sigh of relief. Was saying that in front of the *cadastre* sort of like saying it in court? Could he figure out that he actually did have a legal claim to our house and change his mind? I was tempted to ask Gégé for one of his cigarettes.

"Yes, well...you see there has been an error somewhere along the line," the surveyor explained. "Legally it could be argued that part of this house is yours."

I wanted to grab a dishtowel and muzzle the man.

Monsieur De Luca glanced up at me and gave me a rueful smile that quite transformed his face. "That does not change the fact that this house is not mine and never has been. What must be done to set it right?"

The *cadastre* straightened his spine proudly, taking credit for this swift and amicable resolution. He drew some red lines on the plan he had in front of him, and then scribbled something indecipherable at the bottom.

"Can you just sign here then?" He pushed the paper towards our florid neighbour who shrugged his belligerence at such a stupid mistake, scribbling his name in a signature that was as small and cramped as he was large and imposing.

"French civil servants, eh?" He winked at me. The room seemed full of oxygen once again.

Franck took out the bottle of *cassis* from beside the fridge.

"*Apéro* anyone?"

The surveyor left our abode almost as flushed as Monsieur De Luca, who had departed only five minutes before because, in his words, some of us had real jobs and did not have time to sit around all day fixing the mistakes of notaries and *cadastres, dios mio*!

"You'll need to go back to your notary and sign a rectified Act of Sale," the *cadastre* reminded us in parting.

"You have Monsieur De Luca's signature on the rectified plans, isn't that enough?" I asked.

He shook his head. "*Hélas*, no. That would be far too simple for French administration. I'll send him the documents and he'll call and set up an appointment."

"Actually, he won't," Franck said. "But I'll call and harass him until he does.'

"Who's your notary?" Le Cadastre asked.

"Maître Lefebvre."

The *cadastre* sent us a pitying look as he slid into his seat. "My condolences."

It had taken us two weeks to manage to: a) harass the *cadastre* into sending the rectified plans to the notary and b) harass the notary's secretary into making an appointment with him so we could finalize this thing once and for all. During that time, Franck and Gégé finished eviscerating our walls. More exciting yet, a week after the *cadastre* deigned to grace us with his presence, Gégé informed us one morning that he needed to go down to Beaune to fetch Paulo the plasterer.

"He's Portuguese," Gégé reminded us again as he searched his coat pockets for his car keys.

"So?" I shrugged.

"He doesn't keep his tongue in his pocket."

I frowned at Gégé. "I should hope not."

"It means he talks a lot," Franck helped me out.

"Go get him," I said to Gégé. "I'm sure we have a few pairs of earplugs kicking around here."

Gégé hadn't exaggerated. Paulo's voice made its entrance to our house well before his body. The lyrical sing-song rang through the single paned glass in the far bedroom where I was working. It did not pause for breath and seemed to be telling a series of jokes.

The veranda door clattered and Paulo's voice got louder. I came out of the bedroom and found myself face to face with its owner. He was small and sinewy with deeply tanned skin. He kept prattling to Gégé even as Franck introduced us and continued as we gave each other *les bises*.

Franck ushered us all into the kitchen. The tour of the holes in the walls couldn't start, of course, until we had been served an *apéritif*. The fact that it was ten thirty in the morning was no deterrent in Burgundy.

After knocking back two *kirs* and regaling us with many stories about people we had never met and probably never would, Paulo seemed to have forgotten all about the holes and showed no intention of pausing in his monologue.

Franck managed to slip in the word *les murs* with a questioning finger and beckoned Paulo into the living room. On the way, Paulo regaled us with the tale of how he had just gotten the best deal in the world on his new car – a flashy type of Peugeot – by scaring the car dealer into thinking he was part of the Portuguese mob.

"As if there even is such a thing!" Paulo slapped his muscular thigh. "You should have seen his face though! I swear to you – pale as an *endive!*" Reminiscing about the car dealer turning the same shade as a bulb of chicory, Paulo set off into gales of laughter.

Franck opened the door to the living room and brought Paulo's laughter to an abrupt halt.

He wordlessly surveyed the cavities in the walls. A minute ago I would have given anything for him to shut up but now I wanted nothing more than for him to say something…anything. Franck reached over and grabbed my hand. We waited.

"It's bad, isn't it?" Franck asked.

"I've never seen anything like it," Paulo murmured, then fell silent again.

Franck cracked every one of his knuckles, one by one. "What should we do?"

Paulo pursed his lips, still unable to tear his eyes away from the walls. "Sell the house."

"Too late for that," I said.

Paulo grimaced. "When do you need this done by?"

Franck didn't need as much as a millisecond to calculate exactly how much time we needed. We woke up every morning with a huge neon sign in our minds counting down to Mayday – a word that took on a new and sinister double meaning with each day that passed. "Two and a half months until our first clients arrive."

Paulo lifted his heavy brows and stared at us for a long while.

"*Allez* Paulo," Gégé nudged him. "Tell us what we need to do."

Paulo turned back to the wall and ran his fingers over the closest pockmarked section. He sighed. "Seeing as you will be hanging new wallpaper up I suppose it doesn't need to be *perfect* underneath."

"We're not putting up wallpaper," Franck said. "We're painting."

Paulo turned to Franck. "*Impossible!*"

I gave Franck a small nod – permission to go ahead and rat me out. "Laura doesn't like wallpaper."

Paulo ran his fingers along the crumbling edge of one of the biggest holes that I had decided a few days ago looked rather like Greenland. "It's going to be ten times the work if you want to paint. It has to go from *this*" - he shook his head, despairing - "to *parfait*. You know Laura, they make some very pretty wallpaper."

The three men watched me, waiting for me to concede. I knew there was some very nice wallpaper out there, but I knew even more that I didn't want wallpaper.

"It has to be paint," I said. I didn't relish telling them this but I was certain that my vision of this house just didn't include wallpaper. I couldn't remember the last time I had felt so sure about something.

Paulo let out a guttural noise. "*Vous les femmes!* I should know better than to try and change the mind of a woman when it comes to decorating. You do realize though, that your husband will probably want to divorce you after plastering this room?"

Franck nudged me. "You should listen to Paulo. I'm sure he knows what he's talking about."

"I don't want a divorce," I said. "But it still has to be paint."

Franck turned to Paulo. "What can I do? I made the mistake of marrying a woman with *caractère*." A woman with spirit. It had been a long time since I had thought of myself in that way but this house had a way of bringing out the pluck in me.

Paulo studied me with a mix of annoyance and begrudging respect. "I can see that. I will help you Franck. Us men must stick together."

Paulo, unfortunately for us, had a full-time job in a metal factory in Nuits-Saint-Georges. Plastering was just something he did on the side. Technically, Gégé had a full-time job too, but this never seemed to prevent him from coming to us almost every day, all day. But then again Gégé was a civil servant and Paulo was not. It was agreed over a few more *kirs* – we all needed to sooth our nerves after the paint versus wallpaper stand-off in the living room – that Paulo could come for a few weekends and show Franck the ropes. Paulo made it clear, however, that once he had imparted the art of plastering, Franck would be mainly on his own.

By the time our scheduled appointment with our Notary finally rolled around, Paulo still hadn't come back. Something had cropped up that first weekend, but we were keeping our fingers crossed that he could make it in two days' time.

We got ready to head down to Nuits-Saint-Georges to meet with Maître Lefebvre right after lunch.

"Two o'clock appointment?" Gégé checked his watch. "Not ideal."

Franck pulled on his coat. "*Je sais.* I'm sure most days even he is not sure if he is capable of returning to his office after lunch."

We made the amateur mistake of arriving punctually. When we had waited for forty-five minutes, squirming on the hard plastic chairs, I had to admit Franck was right when he had insisted there was no rush to eat quickly and get to Maître Lefebvre on time. I glanced up at him from the notary newsletter I was skimming. A murderous gleam had begun to take shape in his eyes. To distract him, I slid out my notebook that contained the various lists I had scribbled down the day before.

First there was "Work Completed". It felt like we had been working on the house for countless weeks already yet written down in stark black and white we hadn't actually made that much progress. We had divested the walls of their wallpaper, dug out all the rotten bits of plaster, and made the executive decision that the turquoise bathroom fixtures would have to go.

My second list was "Work To Be Completed". It took up a whole page and I still hadn't finished when I gave up halfway down a second page. It included: re-plastering, installing new bathroom fixtures and wall tile, ripping out old kitchen cabinets, installing new kitchen cabinets, figuring out (and installing) a better heating system, painting the walls, painting most of furniture…and it didn't end there.

It was troubling to be sure, but at least it had the power of momentarily distracting Franck. He twisted a *Paris Match* in his powerful hands, perhaps imagining it was Le Maître's neck, but still, his eyes made their way down my list. Maybe this was not the best time to mention that I had received two more bookings in the past week. It *was* very exciting for me; every booking felt like a triumph. However, based on my lists, every booking also reinforced the reality that we were setting ourselves up for an impossible task.

"You forgot about the *fenêtres*," Franck said.

"Right." I scribbled down *fenêtres* on the "Work To Be Completed" list. A few months ago I would have scribbled down the English word "windows" but now my mind was filled day and night with French words relating to renovations: *plâtre, carrelage, toilettes, plomberie, peinture.* When I was forced into remedial tutoring for my hideous French mark in grade eleven I never would have imagined that ten years later I would be sitting in a French notary's office with my French husband mulling over a French list of the renovations for our French House.

"The windows are in terrible shape," Franck ruminated. "They're drafty and the wood is rotting. They'll all have to be replaced. A friend of my parents is in the window business."

"Really?" This sounded hopeful. "What's his name?"

"Antoine."

"Can you call him?"

Franck eyed the door to the office, which had still not been graced with the Maître's presence. It was going on three o'clock. "I'm not sure if I'll be allowed to make calls from jail," he muttered. "That's where they put you when you kill a notary, *n'est-ce pas?*"

Just then Le Maître blew in the door, hair unkempt and his face a vivid shade of scarlet. Without even sparing a glance at the waiting area – a skill he had no doubt honed over years of practice – he shouted something belligerent to his secretary and then slammed his office door behind him.

Franck stood up. The air around him crackled with anger. The secretary took one knowing glance at him, saw a client that was on the verge of exploding, and pressed the intercom button to talk to the Maître.

"Madame et Monsieur Germain have been waiting since two o'clock," she said. "They have another appointment afterwards," she lied. "Can you see them immediately?"

Muffled raillery followed from Le Maître. Clearly he didn't know or, when I considered the matter more closely, didn't *care* that he was on speakerphone.

"*Bon, d'accord*," he finally acquiesced. "Let them in." He let out a sigh of such epic proportions that I heard it not only through the speakerphone but also through the closed door of his study. Franck didn't need any further invitation. He marched into Le Maître's *étude*.

"*Vous êtes très en retard*. You are very late," Franck said to Le Maître, who froze on his way from his desk to the door to let us in. For a few seconds, Le Maître woozily tried to meet Franck's baleful look with one equally as challenging, then his shoulders dropped and he began to chuckle.

Franck and I weren't sure how to react. We had been primed for a fight, not dissipation.

"Sit down. Please, do sit down." He waved us into the two chairs and picked up a letter from his desk and waved it in the air. "You absolutely must listen to this letter I received this morning."

"Is it from the *cadastre*?" I asked, hopeful.

Le Maître frowned at me as though I was speaking gibberish and began to read: "*You are not only a competent man, but a very alluring one. You know my husband doesn't care for anything now save his tractor and his vines. I find myself a very lonely woman, especially in my intimate life. Could we not find time to get to know each other better?*"

"*Ça alors!*" Le Maître Lefebvre slapped the missive on his desk and surrendered to mirth. "Can you believe it?" Franck and I exchanged a look of bewilderment. Could our notary actually be sharing a love letter with us? "She's practically begging me to sleep with her." He wiped his eyes.

"Will you take her up on it?" Franck asked him, finally. How had we gotten so completely off topic?

Le Maître picked up his Mont Blanc and caressed it, contemplating Franck's question. "I would have to be very desperate. She has no breasts to speak of." With this he looked pointedly at my ample frontage and raised an approving eyebrow at Franck. "No, she is a *vieille peau*," he concluded with regret. "Still her letter is just too funny not to be enjoyed. I read it to my secretary before lunch but as you have seen for yourself she has no sense of humor."

Given the daily aggravation of working with Maître Lefebvre, I felt nobody could really blame her on this point.

"Now then." He smiled magnanimously at us. "What are you here for today?"

It took a good hour plus several exasperated visits from Le Maître's secretary before we were able to rectify the plan so that it actually reflected the house Le Maître had sold us. Le Maître was excessively bored by the proceedings and at several junctures had to go back and quote his favourite passages from his love letter out loud to keep from nodding off.

"And your neighbor agreed to this without any bribery or threats?" Le Maître asked as we were signing the last few documents. He cocked an eyebrow at me. "You didn't offer yourself up to him, did you?"

"I didn't want the house that badly."

He hooted and then, with a beatific smile, began tapping his adding machine to calculate the myriad of different fees that we were going to be charged for his services. After he presented us with a shocking bill, Franck wrote him a cheque. At last we were in possession of documents proving we owned the entirety of our French house.

"I didn't think such a level of unprofessionalism existed," I mused as we climbed back into the car.

"He *was* drunk, you know," Franck said as though this went some way in excusing Le Maître's erratic behaviour.

One of the central ideas I had learned about the law in the past two years was that it had to be taken seriously: you had to take your clients seriously, you had to take yourself seriously, and you had to take your vocation seriously. Le Maître seemed to have missed that lesson entirely. He was, however, living by the Père Bard's credo that God put us all here to have fun....and drink copious amounts of wine.

"I know he's useless as a Notary," Franck admitted. "But you have to admit, he *is* entertaining."

I couldn't argue with that. I rolled down the window and took a deep breath of air that felt as icy as the frost on the vines we whipped past. The house and the furniture in it were finally completely, unequivocally, ours. Now all we needed to do was get it in picture perfect shape for our first guests who were arriving in two months and five days.

I closed my eyes and enjoyed how the soft winter light filtered orange under my eyelids. All we could do was plunge ahead and hope that whoever had been guiding us this far wouldn't abandon us now.

CHAPTER 21

It was the beginning of March. Paulo had come and given his inaugural plastering lesson to Franck and then left him to figure it out on his own. This involved lots of swearing and endless trips down to Beaune to buy bags of dried plaster.

I hopped into the car to accompany Franck down on one such trip. The day before Gégé had also given us an indecipherable list of pipes, taps, and joints to purchase, but my secret plan was to begin perusing for bathroom tile while Franck lost himself in the plumbing section.

Le Gégé had become a member of our little family, or *notre tribu* as Gégé liked to call us. We were living like a strange isolated tribe; all three of us spangled in plaster dust, dreaming of electrical radiators, and unable to relate very well to the rest of humanity. It niggled at me that we had never officially discussed with Gégé how much we were going to pay for his help.

"We need to ask Gégé for an estimate for all the work he's doing," I said to Franck as we sped along *La Nationale* past the shiny yellow and black tiled roof of the castle in Aloxe-Corton. I knew the money was leaking out of our bank account every day and our budget was getting smaller and smaller. I had regular nightmares about getting to the end of work without a single *franc* left to pay our ever-increasing debt.

Franck sped up to pass a vineyard tractor puttering along the road. "Laura, it's not going to happen for a long time, if it happens at all."

"But we *have* to know how much he wants."

"He would be offended if we started talking about money now. You don't want him to leave us, do you?"

"Of course not. I don't know what we'd do without him." Gégé had become the wry rudder of our crazy project and was an invaluable resource and sounding board. Without him, we would be back at square one.

"You'll have to trust me then. We can't ask him about money now. I'll know when the time is right."

I crossed my arms and frowned out the window as the chateau of Clos Vougeot and some of the world's most prized vineyards whizzed by. This did nothing to alleviate my stress, or tie up one of the many loose ends. Anger flared up my neck. Again I was frustrated that I had no choice but to do things Franck's way, especially as I had a hunch that Franck might be wrong. Surely Gégé wanted to know how much he was being paid too. He couldn't be spending day and night helping us for free.

Franck read my silence perfectly. "I'm not wrong about this, you know."

"Hmph."

"It's hard for you to accept that some things will just resolve themselves without your help, isn't it?"

"There's no guarantee that things will resolve themselves on their own." I took my glasses off and picked plaster specks off my lenses.

"Is anything ever truly guaranteed?"

"Don't go all Jean-Paul Sartre on me."

"You could do with a little more French philosophy and a little fewer control needs."

Franck could be annoying, especially when he was right. Still, I couldn't help feeling uneasy about digging a debt hole with Gégé that we might never be able to repay. I liked him too much to fall out over something like that.

At the home renovation store I narrowed my tile choices down to two: a stone coral or a more neutral white with grey wiggles. I meandered back to find Franck in the plumbing section. In front of an impressive display of toilets, Franck was chatting with one of our neighbours from Magny, a winemaker who I had only ever heard referred to as *La Patate* or "The Potato".

In small Burgundian villages like Villers-la-Faye and Magny-les-Villers almost everybody had a nickname. I ruminated on this fact as we sped back to Magny, our trunk almost scraping the road under the weight of several bags of plaster and a mysterious assortment of pipes and joints.

When we got back home I was surprised to see that Gégé hadn't arrived yet. I poured myself a cup of coffee and waited for him by the kitchen window, contemplating how the March wind rattled the bare branches of the two *tilleul* trees across the street. The reconverted Parisian bus used by *Le Jacky* as a mobile shop squealed to a halt in front of the church.

Another neighbor, *La Grenouille* (The Frog) came staggering down the road to buy a baguette from the bus accompanied by his friend *Le Bud*. One of *Le Bud's* hastily pulled up suspenders slipped down as he broke into a trot. *Le Zech* zoomed by in his car and honked and waved at Jacky's bus. Gégé's white *camionette* pulled up and I watched as he got out – he was moving slowly today for some reason - and ambled over to shake hands with *Le Bud* and *La Grenouille* and smoke a companionable cigarette with them. Gégé had begun to refer to Franck as *Le Fou*, "The Crazy". Franck's childhood nickname had begun to stick again – no doubt because he had married a demented Canadian woman who had convinced him to purchase this disaster of a house.

Everyone had a nickname, it seemed. Everyone except me.

I would have settled for a simple "*La*" in front of my name. In these Burgundian villages most people had earned the designation of *Le* or *La* (for example, *La Josette*) in front of their nickname, sort of like the Scottish "Himself". It was not only a way of expressing playful affection for that person, but also a way of recognizing that he or she was irreplaceable, one of a kind. Even though there were about three Josettes in the village, there was only one *La Josette*.

I scratched the fine layer of white plaster dust off the windowpane with my nail. Franck had gotten to the finishing coat of plaster in the living room and had begun his first attempt at sanding the day before. It had taken him two weeks to get to this point in one room and he still wasn't satisfied with the result. I hoped he would pick up speed as we still had all the other rooms left to do.

Gégé bid the men good-bye with another handshake and began to walk over to the passageway under our house. I poured him a coffee while wondering just what it would take for people here to accept me as one of their own and start calling me "*La Laura*", or better yet to be referred to as "*La*" and then to have a nickname bestowed on me as well. It probably would never happen. After all, I wasn't from these villages. The couple from Paris who moved to Villers-la-Faye twenty-five years ago were still referred to as "The Parisians".

So far nobody called me anything but a respectful "Laura" or worse yet, "Madame Germain." They probably referred to me as "*La Canadienne*" as well but never within my earshot.

"*Bonjour*, Laura." Gégé had let himself into the kitchen, the usual brown paper package of croissants and *pain au chocolat* under his arm. We kissed each other on the cheeks and he passed me a *pain au chocolat*. Franck came in, gave me a kiss, and shook Gégé's hand.

We all sat down for a late breakfast and within seconds our patisseries were speckled in plaster dust. Now that the sanding of the walls was well underway there was no escaping the fine white powder that settled on every surface. Gégé had informed us three days ago that he was actually shitting plaster when he went to the WC. I was too afraid to look.

"I'm still sanding." Franck grimaced. "It's harder than it looks and some of the plaster still isn't dry enough."

"Can't we just throw some drywall up in front of all the holes?" I asked for the umpteenth time. I felt like we had been in this plastering stage for a century already.

Gégé shook his head and picked at his croissant. "I've told you Laura, it will start to bubble and weep within months. It would be like stitching up an abscess before draining it first."

I was so put off by this analogy that I put down my pastry.

"You don't look very good this morning." Franck studied Gégé. "Are you feeling all right?"

"I'm depressed," Gégé answered, picking at his croissant.

This got my attention. Maybe it was the gray March skies, but I had also been feeling despair lurking around the edges of life the past few days.

"About what?" Franck asked.

Gégé gave the saddest shrug I had ever seen. "Everything."

"Everything what?" Franck probed.

Gégé took a drag on his cigarette and his eyes teared up. He tried to laugh but it came out as a gulp. "Where should I start?"

"Start with the thing that is bothering you the most," Franck said.

He looked down at the table top, his chin quivering. "I want to have a girlfriend. I see you two together and I want that. I've been lonely for so long. Olivier and everyone say it's going to happen any day now, that I'm going to meet someone, but *merde!* Where is she? I'm starting to think that there's nobody. I'll be lonely forever."

I sat perfectly still in my chair, riveted. Didn't Gégé know that adults weren't supposed to admit to feelings like that, even to themselves?

"Olivier sat across from me a few years ago saying the exact same thing as you," Franck pointed out. "Now he's married and has a son."

Gégé's mouth twisted. "Just because it happened to Olivier doesn't mean it's going to happen to me. Is it because I keep making the wrong choices? I mean, look at me. No girlfriend, no place of my own, not a lot of money…what is the point of it all? I'm completely lost."

I gasped. Even at my most discouraged, I could never bring myself to actually admit to the feeling. I had always assumed that feeling lost meant something was defective with *me* because weren't we supposed to feel happy all the time?

However, I didn't think Gégé was at all defective for feeling depressed. Instead, I was impressed by his courage in admitting how he really felt, even though it scared me. It made me feel as though he were dangling me over a cliff. If I followed his brave example – which I longed to – I would surely drown in years of pent-up emotions.

Large tears began to roll down Gégé's cheeks. I didn't know where to look and stared down as I began to dissect my *pain au chocolat*. Franck, being from a family who aired its emotional distress with the same nonchalance as t-shirts on the laundry line, munched through his second croissant while watching Gégé, concerned but nonplussed.

"Tell me some of your problems," Gégé said after a few minutes of crying. "*S'il vous plaît.* That way I won't feel so alone."

"The walls," Franck said, his voice muffled with pastry. "I dream about those holes every night. Most nights I get up to look at them to see if they are really as big and as bad as they are in my nightmares, only to find that they are actually worse. Then I can't get back to sleep for a long time afterwards. I'm also scared that we're running out of time, not to mention money."

Gégé nodded sympathetically and his brown eyes shifted to me. "*Et toi?*"

I blinked. Everything felt wrong! I felt utterly overwhelmed, but I couldn't say it. I had to keep it in, didn't I? Wasn't that my penance for having these feelings in the first place?

"Don't get me started!" I laughed, taking the coward's way out. "The holes, of course, and the other things Franck said."

Gégé watched me for a few more seconds than was polite. He didn't buy it. Thankfully he pushed back his chair and beckoned to Franck. "We can't do much about my problems today, but let's see if we can't do something about those holes."

A few days later, Franck had rounded up as many muscular friends and family as possible to help move the turquoise fixtures out of our bathroom. Gégé reported for duty the morning of the move.

"*Ça va?*" I asked as I did every morning.

"Still depressed," he informed me, as he had done every morning since he had broken down at our breakfast table. He said it in a resigned, matter-of-fact way, as though reporting the weather.

I had felt strangely on guard around him since that first morning. I tried to convince myself that it was merely because I wasn't as comfortable sharing negative emotions as a French person, but the truth was that my unease went deeper. I was jealous of him.

It was clear that he never even considered for a moment trying to hide his depression. To actually admit to the distressing feelings that often spun inside me...it would be so freeing, so indulgent, so...terrifying. I was certain in that deep, visceral spot inside my soul that the universe would cave in if I dared. I was jealous of Gégé's courage and jealous of the freedom that his courage bought him. I knew he wouldn't understand this.

That morning, like the past few mornings, I found myself circling warily around Gégé, desperate for him to ask me what was wrong and dreading that he would.

Luckily Franck's father and Olivier and Martial arrived and in a wave of testosterone everyone swept into the bathroom and removed all of the turquoise fixtures in under half an hour. Gégé complained the most about the weight of the cast iron bathtub yet he was actually the happiest I had seen him in a long time, joking and egging the others on.

I was smiling as they drove off to the dump but as I went back inside and surveyed my now empty bathroom my smile vanished. The stained wallpaper around the edges of the holes reminded me that everything we were doing here would eventually be undone by time or by new owners. Everyone died in the end. What was the point of it all?

My breath couldn't seem to come fast enough; nausea climbed up my throat. This was all terribly wrong. Something catastrophic was going to happen because of the choices I had made.

I stumbled outside and took gulps of air yet couldn't seem to fill my lungs. I didn't think I could bear this panic for one second longer. I lowered myself to the top step. I was certain that at any second the universe was going to cave in and it would be *entirely my fault*. Black spots danced in front of my eyes. I was certain I would suffer like this forever. The anxiety kept subsiding for a few moments, then rushing forward again in waves, each one more disorienting than its predecessor. I clutched my chest.

Gégé's whistle came around the corner. I knew I needed to escape inside but I couldn't seem to move.

"There was a man at the dump who took everything!" I heard him say but his voice came through to me as though he were above water and I below.

I raised my head.

One look at me and his expression of delight melted away.

"What's wrong Laura? Do you need me to call the doctor?"

"*Non*...Yes..." I gasped. "I don't know. I don't know...it's just...so stressful."

Then Gégé, a shy man who seemed to have to gear himself up for the touching required by our daily *bises*, placed his hand on my shoulder.

"I know," he said. I still couldn't look at him. The panic began to ebb, only to be replaced by excruciating embarrassment.

"Laura," he ordered, "Look at me." I did. His brown eyes were full of understanding.

"I just..."

"I *know*," he said. I knew then I had never needed to tell him anything. He knew exactly how I felt and he had felt that way too. The fact that I wasn't alone meant everything in that moment. I burst into tears. I sobbed so hard that I had to cling to the cold metal railing for support. Gégé didn't try to hug me or tell me to stop. He just rubbed my shoulder and murmured "I know" over and over again.

"It's hard being alive sometimes, *n'est-ce pas?*" Gégé said when my tears began to subside.

I nodded and took a shuddering breath.

"He was thrilled with the bidet."

I wiped my eyes, confused. "Who?"

"A man at the dump ended up taking all the fixtures home with him. He was thrilled with the turquoise bidet in particular." The thought managed to bring a little smile to my face, and it was reflected in Gégé's.

"I guess that's something."

"It *is* something," he said. "The others will be coming back soon. Do you need to go and blow your nose?"

"Yeah." I scrubbed my face with my hands to try and even out the splotches. "*Merci* Gégé. Maybe we could keep…"

"*Ne fais pas du souci.*" He gave my shoulder a final pat. "No one will know there was anything amiss with *La Lolo*. We all find life hard sometimes."

It wasn't until I went into the WC to blow my nose that I realized Gégé hadn't called me Laura. He had called me "*La Lolo*." My new nickname.

CHAPTER 22

The day after the bathroom had been stripped of its turquoise fittings and I had earned a nickname not by being strong, but by being vulnerable, Franck informed me that he had invited Gégé, *Le Paulo*, and an electrician they called Momo over for dinner the next night.

I surveyed our kitchen, which was covered in plaster dust and had frayed electrical cables hanging from the holes Franck and Gégé had excavated in the ceiling.

"Are you insane?" I asked.

"A bit," he admitted. "But I may need to call Paulo in to help again if we're going to get the plastering back on track and" - he pointed up at the dangling cables overhead - "I think you'll agree with me that we need an electrician sooner rather than later. Thierry has a friend named Momo who's an electrician. We're going over to their place tonight to get the information and I want Momo to be at the dinner too."

I turned around to the kitchen again. "How are we supposed to cook in this mess? Can't we just take them out to a restaurant?"

Franck shook his head. His usually black hair was almost white. "That's not the way it's done in Burgundy. It would be an insult."

I ran my hand through Franck's hair, unleashing a shower of fine white dust. "More of an insult than feeding them chunks of plaster in their food?"

Franck nodded. "Definitely."

Renovation-wise I had less to do than Franck who was up to his ears in plastering, so I knew the onus was on me to feed the guests at dinner the next night. This was Burgundy, where sublime food and wine counted more than life itself. If my cooking was bad we might, in all seriousness, be abandoned by our helpers for good.

"You'd better plan on serving lots of wine." I pulled down Franck's T-shirt and found a clean spot of skin on his collarbone to kiss.

"You can count on that." He swatted me on the bottom with his trowel. *"Merci, mon amour."*

Momo, we learned that night at Stéph and Thierry's house, was an electrician who lived two villages over and was a childhood friend of Thierry, Stéphanie's husband. In the village, Momo went by two nicknames. In polite circles his actual name Maurice was shortened to "Momo," but his friends knew him as *L'âne* or "the donkey".

"Is it because he's stubborn?" I asked. We had been in front of the fireplace and Tom was crawling around us, executing laborious u-turns every time he bumped into our legs.

Thierry smirked. "Ah...*non.*"

"Why then?"

Franck caught Thierry's eye and the two of them started to laugh.

"Quoi?" I didn't like the idea of having this donkey person fool around with our electrical cables until I knew the whole story.

"Have you ever seen a donkey?" Thierry asked.

"Bien sûr. My grandmother used to have one on her farm. His name was Tex and we used to try to feed him carrots and stuff. He would spit at us. He died eventually and we buried him under my grandmother's apple tree. He was a nasty, spiteful thing. He used to bite us all the time. Three years later my cousins and I pretended that we were archaeologists and dug up all his bones."

Thierry shot a mystified look at Franck, not sure quite what to do with my impromptu walk down memory lane.

"Did you ever see the donkey...you know, excited?" Frank asked me.

I thought about this for a moment. "I don't think so. There were no female donkeys around, just a lot of sheep." The coin dropped. There *had* been two horses, Areeb and Pal, and I had definitely seen them. If donkeys were anything like horses…Franck and Thierry hooted with laughter.

"*D'accord.* I get it now." I waved my hand at them to shut up. "Is that really true about our electrician?"

Franck stopped laughing. "What kind of question is that?"

"*Allez.* I bet you want to know the answer too."

"I certainly do not."

I raised a brow at Thierry. "Is it true?"

Thierry took another sip of his *kir.* "Just ask any woman who lives in these villages. "

"You don't seriously mean he shows it off when he's making house calls?"

"Laura!" Franck said.

"He's quite well known for seducing his female customers," Thierry admitted.

Franck frowned at Thierry. "You couldn't have told me this before?"

"I thought you knew." Thierry protested with a shrug. "Everybody around here knows."

"I didn't hear that part of it. You just told me that he fenced in his free time and almost made it onto the Olympic team when he was younger."

Thierry raised an eyebrow. "What better way to defend himself against all the angry husbands?"

The next morning Franck got up in a chipper mood, but by the time lunch rolled around his cheery humour had been defeated by the challenge of making a smooth surface of our horribly ancient and humid walls.

As we sat down over a *salade frisée*, a roll of parma ham each and a round of camembert, I saw that my husband was glaring at the world through an *oeil noir*.

"*Ça va?*" I ventured but he merely frowned and wiped his hands on his plaster spackled jeans. Apparently, now that Gégé and I were emerging from our respective funks, it was Franck's turn. The timing couldn't have be worse, I reflected as I sat down over my after lunch café and sucked my pencil, wracking my brain to come up with something I could cook for Gégé, Paulo, and Momo that night in our tiny kitchen. It had to be something strong tasting and dark in colour so that the inevitable plaster in the dish would remain undetected.

"Do you have any ideas for dinner?" I asked Franck who nursed his coffee across from me.

"*Non.*"

He was definitely in what I always thought of as one of his *French* moods. His whole family indulged in them on occasion, as did pretty much every French person I knew. The Canadians I had grown up with most definitely did not. Not in public anyway. Maybe this was why I still felt a strange mix of embarrassment and relief when I thought about breaking down in front of Gégé.

"You seem to be in a bad mood," I observed, trying to keep my tone light. In general I tried to keep a sense of humour about Franck's French moods but after a while they never failed to destabilize me. I wasn't sure where it came from, but deeply embedded in my brain was the conviction that I should be able to make everyone around me happy.

"I'm fine."

When Franck was in one of his rare funks I knew from experience that nothing I could say or do could pull him out of it.

Gégé came in the kitchen then, took one look at Franck and raised an eyebrow at me.

I shrugged. "I'm trying to figure out what to cook for dinner tonight. Any ideas?"

"*Oui!*" Gégé served himself some coffee. "A couple of smoked *morteau* sausages and potatoes in the pressure cooker with *crème fraiche* and freshly chopped parsley."

"That's perfect! Can you tell me how to make it?"

Gégé did just that, then left Franck and me alone again while he went down to the cellar to examine some pipes.

"Gégé's idea is nothing short of brilliant," I remarked as I marked down *crème fraîche* on my shopping list. The recipe was easy, filling, delicious, and required only two pots.

"I need to get back to those walls." Franck got up and poured the remaining half of his coffee in the sink.

I had to pull off this dinner, surly husband or not.

By the time seven o'clock rolled around I was at my wit's end trying to clear out enough debris in our living room to make room for an empty table and five chairs around it.

The potatoes and the *morteau* had been purchased and were cooking away in our trusty SEB pressure cooker – an essential tool in any self-respecting French kitchen, even the most rudimentary ones like ours. The comforting smell of smoked pork and garlic filled the house. Even the odour of burning rubber from the convection heaters provided no match.

I had poured the *crème fraîche* into a small casserole so that it would be ready to heat up a few minutes before we served the dish.

As I was snipping up my parsley in a glass with scissors - like Mémé had showed me - Franck stomped into the kitchen. He looked around, muttered "*quel bordel!*" then took himself off again. A mess? Of course the kitchen was a mess. There was nowhere for me to put the pots and pans I was using to cook. The whole house was a mess - we were in the middle of renovating it. It wasn't only the pressure cooker that began to steam. We had people coming to dinner though, people whose help we needed. Now wasn't the time for me to explode.

I wrenched open the sticky window and drank in the spring air, hoping it would cool down my temper. The church across the street hunched in front of a restless sky.

Why did my life always seem so much messier than everyone else's?

The door clattered open and Paulo's voice arrived in mid-sentence. I listened for a few seconds as he recounted how a barrel of wine had fallen off a truck in front of his house. I took a last gulp of air and shut the window. These guys were the only ones who could help us out of our fix. Somebody had to be the gracious host and I didn't think it was going to be Franck.

I could tell as I brought the steaming dish of *morteau* sausages and fingerling potatoes into the living room that this evening was going to take every single ounce of tact and diplomacy in me. Paulo was keeping up a constant stream of tall tales. Franck and Gégé, who was dressed in an ironed dress shirt and dress shoes with his best jeans, were a receptive – meaning completely silent - audience. It would have been a relief to stay pinned in my chair by the centrifugal force of Paulo's never-ending monologue. Momo, however, was the problem.

After a few minutes in his company it became clear that this reputedly well-endowed specimen liked to be the centre of attention himself. He, unlike Franck, Gégé, and I was not content to sit back and let Paulo steal the limelight for the evening. The more Paulo talked, the more Momo fidgeted in his chair.

Franck kept our glasses of *Ladoix Premier Cru* topped up but this didn't seem to mellow the two men at all. Rather the contrary, in fact.

"Those Pauland idiots came by every day for a month," Paulo rambled on. "They had bought up every house around me and had all the land to build their new winery. I kept telling them that I couldn't make up my mind and to come back the next - "

"I know the guy who did the electrical for that build," Momo interrupted.

"I had them over a barrel," Paulo turned his voice up a notch, talking right over Momo as he continued to tell his excruciatingly detailed story. "So what I did next was - "

"Do you know what happened to me when I was fencing the other afternoon?" Momo asked us. I stood up and began to clear the plates.

"...tell them I would *never* sell my house to them - " Paulo's voice got even louder.

Momo's eyes kindled. "There was this woman - "

"But they came back the very next day with their lawyer. Can you believe that?"

I scurried off to the kitchen and took a long time assembling my cheese platter of *Époisses*, *Cîteaux*, and *Comté*. When I could avoid it no longer I went back into the living room just in time to hear Momo yell belligerently at Paulo, "I think you could have gotten them to pay you a lot more for your house!"

I stood frozen a few feet from the table. Paulo's muscular forearms flexed. "What did you just say?"

Gégé and I exchanged worried looks. Franck looked mildly interested for the first time since lunch.

"Your story is boring." Momo spread out his sinewy hand on the tablecloth that I had hoped would add a touch of civility to the proceedings. "If you had held on longer you could have got those rich idiots at Pauland to pay you double that amount." I stared at Momo, incredulous. With the exception of Gégé, the men were behaving like little boys in the schoolyard.

Paulo curled his fingers into a fist. "Say that again. Go ahead. Say it!"

I wanted to crawl underneath the table. It reminded me of the time we were having dinner at our newly engaged friends' apartment in Lyon and they embarked on a marital spat of such epic proportions that it ended with the fiancée twisting off her engagement ring, flinging it out the window to the courtyard below and stalking out of the room. I had often wondered if French people felt the compulsion to misbehave in front of me precisely because I was such a well-behaved audience.

"Your story is *n'importe quoi*." Momo tossed this smouldering log on the fire. Franck made no attempt to mediate. On the contrary, his eyes widened with delight at the prospect of a pre-dessert brawl. Paulo knuckled the tabletop and stood up.

"You are a *petit merde*." Oh dear. Not so much the "shit" part but the "little" part. Momo was on the small side, even for a French man.

Gégé threw me a desperate look. We needed them both to keep working with us, but I didn't know what I could do now to save the evening. It was too late.

Momo stood up, cocky as a rooster. I was fed up with Gégé and me being the only well behaved people around. I threw the cheese platter down on the table.

"Stop it!"

Neither Momo nor Paulo seemed to hear me. They remained standing; their eyes did not leave each other. My fist came down hard on the table.

"You should be ashamed of yourselves!"

The four men stared at me and then glanced at each other, not quite sure what to do. Gégé roused himself first and gave me a little grin. Why should I be the one who felt embarrassment when other people were behaving rudely?

"I made you all a nice dinner tonight even though I'm exhausted and the house is a disaster and Franck has been in a funk for most of the day." Paulo opened his mouth but I held up my hand and adopted the French technique of speaking even louder. "All you do is bicker with each other while Franck sits in the corner, enjoying the show. I will not have it! Paulo, Momo, Franck - you have a choice. Either you start behaving or I am going to kick you out of my house!"

I glared at each of them, daring them to talk back. After a moment, Momo and Paulo sat down.

"Gégé, you can stay," I added.

None of them uttered a sound. Gégé caught my eye and made a silent clapping gesture with his hands. The other three men studied the olive branch print of our tablecloth as though it were a lingerie catalogue. Why had I never tried yelling at rude guests before? It was a revelation.

After a minute or two of stony silence Gégé began to chuckle. "What's wrong *les gars*?" he chided his fellow men. "Cat got your tongue?"

Franck looked up at me and cracked a sheepish smile. Paulo and Momo began to laugh as well, and finally relaxed their shoulders.

"Are you going to start behaving yourselves?" I demanded. "Otherwise you will get no dessert from me."

They nodded like schoolboys – obedient schoolboys now.

"*Bien*," I said. "In that case, help yourself to the cheese."

The *Époisses* was creamy and stinky, but it did not even come close to the deliciousness of allowing myself to tell everyone off.

When I glided into the kitchen to get the *tarte aux poires* that I had bought from the *patisserie*, I heard Momo say to Franck, "You've got a real hellion for a wife."

"I know," Franck answered, pride in his voice. "Isn't she great?"

CHAPTER 23

Today we found a possible solution to our window problem. His name is Antoine.

Michèle, Franck's mother, and Antoine met at Lourdes several years previously while Michèle was searching for a miracle to cure her cancer. Antoine was a volunteer there. He became not only a close friend but also one of Michèle's pillars of support during her treatment and recovery. When he wasn't busy facilitating miracles on behalf of the Virgin Mary, Antoine - a compact ball of energy with a round head and thin moustache - worked as a window installer.

His personal life had always been a mystery to Franck's family. Like a modern day saint he went through life helping the sick, the desperate, and the lonely; he usually had at least one person recuperating at his home. Franck had warned me early on not to ask too many questions.

"He is from Brittany," Franck said by way of explanation.

"Why can't I ask questions of people from Brittany?"

"A *Breton* will be the best friend you could ever have," Franck said. "But they value their privacy and they have *du caractère*. We must respect that."

Antoine blew into our house three days after our almost disastrous dinner party with Momo and Paulo who, after my chastising, both got sauced and bonded over the extortionate taxes the French government imposed on small business owners and the excellent *Ladoix* Franck was serving (made by one of his many distant cousins, *bien sûr*).

Antoine looked like an eager gnome. His work pants were a well-worn azure and a tool belt of strange looking implements hung around his waist. He surprised me by refusing coffee.

"Work first!" he declared, then sallied into the living room and subjected our weather-beaten living room window to a vigorous inspection. "Disgraceful!" He clicked his tongue. "You must be freezing."

Even though it was now almost April the weather was still unseasonably cold. I looked down and realized I had my arms wrapped around my torso again. I didn't even notice the cold anymore.

"We do what we can to keep ourselves warm." Franck kept an admirably straight face.

Antoine let out a hoot of high-pitched laughter. "Maybe you don't want me to replace them, *hein*?" He took out his tape measure and went from room to room measuring and making note of all of the windows that needed replacing - the three along the front looking out to the church and then two tiny ones up in the attic.

Franck and I exchanged worried looks as Antoine scribbled on his paper. I thought back to our budget meeting of the night before as we lay in bed, and began to run through how much money we had to finish and the corresponding list of things still to do.

The harsh reality was that we only had twenty five thousand francs left. It sounded like a lot, but really it only amounted to a little more than five thousand dollars. We had thought we would save a lot of money by Franck plastering the walls by himself, but the holes were so deep and so plentiful that we found ourselves buying new bags of plaster every day. Each bag didn't cost that much but they added up. Still, we knew that we had no choice but to replace our windows. They were rotting, after all. We also knew that this would prove to be an expensive proposition – Gégé took exquisite pleasure in reminding us of this fact several times a day.

"So, how much do you think they will cost?" Franck asked Antoine. Just then Gégé, with his unerring radar for catastrophe, sauntered in from the bathroom where he had been busy installing the new fixtures.

Antoine tucked the pencil behind his ear and studied his notepad. "I think it will come to about fifteen thousand francs."

That was a huge chunk of our remaining budget. It would leave us with only ten thousand francs to finish the rest. A pittance.

"*Merde.*" Franck's index finger twitched. "That was more than I was hoping for. Does the price include installation?"

Antoine grinned at our worried expressions and slapped Franck on the shoulder. "*Ne t'en fais pas*. I can do the installation. I'll just need to add a little extra for my materials, silicone for the joints and such."

"*Merci*," I said. It was generous of him. Maybe the Virgin Mary really had sent him to perform her miracles on earth.

"They would not be our top-of-the-line windows, you understand," Antoine said. "But they are really the minimum of what is required in an old house like this. So should I add up the total? Fifteen thousand francs per window multiplied by three large windows and - "

Franck made a choking noise. "You meant fifteen thousand francs *per* window?"

"But of course! Doing it for any less is *impossible*."

Neither Franck nor I could speak.

Gégé watched us, delight illuminating his narrow face. "The three main floor windows alone would cost almost double the budget you have left for the rest of the house," he calculated. What? He was a math genius all of a sudden?

"*Merci*, Gégé," Franck said through clenched teeth.

"Could we somehow make do with these ones?" I asked, fingering the splintered window frame. A large chunk of wood crumbled off in my hand, answering my question. I turned to Antoine. "We just don't have the money."

Antoine sniffed. "Windows are the most important things you can install when doing renovations. Windows are always where you should go high end."

"But we can't afford to go high end anywhere." I tried to make him understand.

"The price I quoted you is the price for the least expensive window that our company manufactures." From his huffy expression I knew I was raising the ire of his *Breton* blood.

"What about going with windows from a different company?" Gégé suggested. "I know a lot of people that have installed windows from that store Lapeyre on the route de Dijon. They seem fine."

Antoine turned the same shade of crimson as a young *Pommard* wine. "*Eh oui*, Lapeyre windows are just fine if what you like is *la merde*! They are the McDonalds of windows! The joints are made in China and the wood will warp in twenty years!" He shook his fist at the infamy of Gégé's suggestion. Ah…here was the Breton *caractère* Franck had warned me about.

Frankly, Gégé's suggestion sounded wonderful. Franck sent me a look that told me he felt the same.

"I could live with the windows warping twenty years from now," he said, finally.

"So could I." Maybe in twenty years' time we would actually afford to get new windows from Antoine's company, but these renovations had a way of transforming me into a *carpe diem* kind of person.

Gégé tried, unsuccessfully, to stifle a grin of triumph.

"Fine!" Antoine ripped out his measuring tape and began to measure the window as if it was his mortal enemy. He scribbled something else on a fresh sheet of paper and shoved it over to Franck. "These are the measurements you'll need to order. Call me when they've arrived and I'll come and install them. I warn you now though; I can't make any promises with such inferior materials." He began to storm out of the living room, but caught sight of our mammoth stone fireplace.

"What are you going to do with that fireplace?" he demanded.

Franck folded up the paper carefully and slipped it in his back pocket. "We can't afford to refurbish the chimney and even if we did it would still be a fire hazard that would affect our insurance. We had the idea of making some sort of bookshelf in there but we have to find a carpenter."

"And more money," I added.

Franck nodded. "And more money."

Antoine raised his eyes to the heavens. "Find a carpenter! Why would you do that when you've got me?" He took out his measuring tape again and, thus armed, accosted the fireplace. "I see that I'll have to stay. You'll never be able to pull this off without me."

I was ready to take salvation in whichever form it arrived, even a volatile *Breton*.

It was official. We had only three weeks left before our first guests arrived. I had discovered, strangely, that all this time I had been harboring a hidden gift for Internet marketing. Incredibly, I had booked twenty groups of guests for our next year. We were now completely booked up from April 30, when our first guests arrived, until the end of November.

My fingers were poised over the keyboard of my makeshift computer station in the corner of the living room. The white plaster walls around me looked smooth and pristine thanks to Paulo coming up the past two days to help Franck. They were almost finished the front bedroom too.

I opened my email and clicked on a message from our first group of guests: *Bonjour Laura! We are gearing up for our trip to France. How are the renovations going? We've bought our tickets now and should be arriving at your house at around 8:00pm on April 30. Can you please send directions and how to find the key? We're getting very excited!*

Today was April 7. Yesterday Franck had bought our train tickets to travel to Oxford, leaving Dijon at 6:12 a.m. on April 30 to get there in time for my graduation ceremony on the morning of May 1 and the festivities of May Day in England. In front of the keyboard I invariably experienced a manic surge of optimism. For those few moments I truly did believe it would be possible to get the house ready for them in time. It was when I stood up and looked beyond my computer screen that my optimism fell down around my feet. I still had to paint the entire house as well as the shutters and some pieces of furniture. Antoine had to install our windows (which had just arrived) and we needed to install our newly purchased electric radiators. The bathroom wall needed to be tiled... May Day. Mayday. Mayday. Mayday. The voice in my head plummeted into a nosedive.

I was dying to begin painting the living room but Franck insisted that the radiators had to be installed first. Besides, he wasn't exactly sure how long the plaster took to dry completely. When he wasn't looking I would run my hand over the silky smooth surface of the new walls, trying to decide on what color paint to choose. Beige didn't tempt me in the slightest. Would I paint the walls the lavender shade of the dusty part of a pinot noir grape? The yellow of the canola fields in full bloom? Or the crisp apple green of the vineyard's leaves when they first unfurled?

Before paint came the radiators and before the radiators could be installed, the windows had to be changed. Antoine, who had gone to Dijon with Franck to pick up the windows from that den of iniquity known as Lapeyre, was now busy installing them. Antoine truly knew his way around a window. He cut, sealed, and wielded the silicone gun with the same nonchalance as a solicitor in London marking up a multi-million dollar contract.

Now that the weather had turned warm I had begun to sand the shutters down in the courtyard. I went back down, plugged in the electric sander and ran it over the peeling white paint of one side of the shutters. When I was done I went back inside to get a glass of water from the kitchen.

I watched as Antoine slipped the new window in the hole made by the old one and anchored it with several little wedges of paper.

I whistled. "You measured that perfectly. I'd never be able to do that."

"You would if you did it all day long, every day."

I wasn't so sure about that. Paying attention to detail actually hurt my brain. This was probably why pouring over obscure contract clauses during my law degree had felt akin to being stretched on the rack.

"Do you like doing it?" I asked.

"Doing what?"

"Installing windows."

He shrugged. "I have to earn money somehow. How else can I buy nice wine and antiques and go out to restaurants? There are a lot of more unpleasant ways to earn money. "

I took a sip of my water. I had always been brought up believing that people *were* their career. They *were* a doctor, or a lawyer, or a real estate agent. In North America, one of the first questions you asked upon meeting someone was, "what do you do?" Of course, what you were really asking was, "what are you?"

Yet here was Antoine, clearly an expert on installing windows but also an expert of so many other things, given our myriad of conversations about French literature and antique furniture and his favourite wines. Installing windows was something he merely did, not who he was.

Maybe I too should just look for a way to earn money that I didn't hate, and which would finance my other pursuits, like sanding shutters and rescuing ancient door hinges.

The little whistle on the pressure cooker began to turn in lazy circles and a delicious honeyed smell filled the kitchen.

"Who..." I started to ask.

"I'm cooking us a *rôti de porc au pruneaux*," Antoine said. A filet of pork with prunes. Yum. "It will be ready at noon. While you're down there sanding, could you grab us a bottle of wine to go with it? One of Claire's *Côte de Nuits* should do nicely. Your window should be installed by the time we uncork the bottle."

It was while we were still mopping up the succulent sauce of Antoine's *rôti* that Momo brought by his employee who would be installing our new radiators. Gégé had been invited to join us for lunch, despite the fact that Antoine still resented him for suggesting he work with inferior materials. This did not seem to hinder Gégé's enjoyment of Antoine's cooking in the slightest. He made grunts of pleasure as he chewed his last sauce-soaked piece of baguette.

Momo let himself into the kitchen, trailed by a mammoth man with an untamed forest of hair on his head and a thicket of a beard. Momo, who stood about five-foot four and was as sinewy as they come, looked as though he could easily be squeezed up into a ball and lobbed out the window by his employee.

"I've brought you your electrician." Momo helped himself to a glass of coffee. He waved in the giant's direction. "Meet Tintin."

"Don't you sit down and eat a proper lunch?" Antoine demanded of the two arrivals without even saying *bonjour*. "We haven't even begun our cheese course yet."

"No," Momo said. Tintin didn't answer, but glanced at our food and then back at Momo resentfully.

Tintin couldn't possibly be his real name unless his parents were completely deranged. Tintin was a comic book hero that French children were weaned on. Our Tintin had virtually no physical similarities with the eternally boyish hero with the blond duckbill of hair of Hergé's comic books. Franck, Antoine and Gégé were all casting sideways glances at our new electrician, surely wondering, like me, how he had earned his sobriquet but asking him directly didn't seem like the smartest idea.

"Would you like a coffee, Tintin?" Franck ventured.

"*Non*," Tintin grunted. "Where are the radiators?"

"A charmer, isn't he?" Momo laughed and slapped Tintin on his hulking back. "He is probably the stupidest of my guys but he was the only one available. *Salut!*" On this parting note, Momo set down his espresso cup and left.

Antoine widened his eyes at me. Had Momo been joking about Tintin being a bad electrician? I didn't know Momo that well. Surely he wouldn't foist his worst electrician on us.

"Are you sure you wouldn't like to sit down with us and have something to eat or drink?" Franck asked again. Tintin cast us a baleful look with flat black eyes that reminded me of a shark.

"No. Momo wants me to start. Where are the radiators?" Franck had no choice but to push back from the table and lead him down to the cellar where the radiators were stored in their boxes.

"What do you think?" Gégé said when they were well out of earshot. "Do you think he's really here to install the radiators or to murder one of us?"

Antoine considered this. "Maybe he's here to murder all of us."

"I'm not sure about Tintin." I got up and started putting together the cheese plate. "But if Momo really sent us his worst electrician, I will definitely murder *him*."

Tintin began working in the front bedroom. There was a tension in the air while he was under the same roof as the rest of us. The few times he spared a glance for one of us on his way outside to smoke a cigarette he looked as though he was contemplating how to dispose of our bodies.

Finally, around six-thirty, he walked out a final time with all his tools.

"*Au revoir* Tintin," Franck called after him. "See you tomorrow!" Tintin grunted.

I ran to the kitchen window and watched as he got in his rusty red car and sped off. "He's gone!"

Franck, Antoine, and Gégé joined me in the front bedroom to inspect Tintin's handiwork.

"*Merde alors*," muttered Franck. Not only had Tintin made a mess of Franck's beautifully plastered and sanded stretch of wall under the window, but instead of centering our expensive rectangular flat radiator in the space below the window he had placed it a mere centimetre or so from the floor itself.

Antoine flushed scarlet. "What is this pig's work!?" He bent down and stuck his finger in the huge cut Tintin had made in the plaster and blew out an angry puff of air. "He has installed it this way because he is a lazy bastard who does not want to re-plaster any more than necessary."

"Are *you* going to tell him that?" Gégé asked Antoine.

Antoine sniffed and stood up. "That is not my place. I am not the homeowner." He cast Franck a loaded glance.

The next morning Tintin arrived at seven thirty and stalked back to the front bedroom without so much as a *bonjour* to the rest of us.

Gégé gave Franck a pat on the back and we all huddled in the kitchen and listened for sounds of carnage as Franck went to talk to Tintin about repositioning the radiator. After what seemed like a very long time Franck came back to us.

"You're still alive!" Gégé said.

Franck shushed him.

"What happened?" Antoine asked. "Did you tell him he worked like a pig?"

Franck rolled his eyes. "Ah. . . .*non*. I put it a little more diplomatically that that. I asked if it would be possible to put the radiator higher up, as I was worried about it being kicked so close to the floor."

I got up and gave Franck a hug for his bravery. "And?" I said. "How did he take it?"

"He wasn't very happy, but I think he'll do it. We'll see."

We had no choice but to go on with our respective work. We all stayed away from Tintin and the bedrooms. I began to prime the first pair of sanded shutters outside. Swallows chirped and the tractors trundled past on their way out to the vineyards. Winter had vacated the premises and the sunshine warming my hair made me feel as though anything was possible.

Tintin's presence was menacing but it united the rest of us. Franck and I stopped arguing about whether the walls were ready to paint or not, and even Gégé and Antoine stopped pushing each other's buttons. Most of the time anyway.

Tintin clearly didn't want to be installing the radiators at our house. I didn't take this personally, as my instinct told me that he didn't want to be installing radiators in anybody's house. He felt no compunction to even pretend that he was happy with the circumstances. His disgust for his job and us was unnerving but I had to admire its honesty.

I dipped my brush in the paint pot again, and brushed the shutter on the sawhorse in front of me.

The last two years during law school I had pretended to be happy out of a sense of obligation to others. It never even occurred to me that I had a choice in the matter. It would have been immensely satisfying to stalk into one of my tutorials and respond to my tutors with grunts, á la Tintin.

Happy might be a big word for how I felt now – of course, I was exhausted and stressed about not getting everything finished – but there was a sense of satisfaction in transforming this dump of a house into something charming and, dare I say it, beautiful. Moreover, working alongside Gégé and Antoine and Franck meant that I was never alone with the daily triumphs and worries. I had always considered myself to be someone who preferred flying solo in my work but now I wasn't so sure.

I fell even deeper into the meditative act of painting and lost track of time until Tintin stalked out of the house with his jacket on, presumably to go to lunch.

"*Bon appétit!*" I said as he passed. He didn't even turn around.

Gégé sprung out the veranda door a few moments later as I was inspecting my shutters for errant bugs stuck in the paint. "You have to see this!"

I followed him into the house, then to the green bedroom where both Antoine and Franck were standing in front of the newly moved radiator, their faces a study of consternation.

"Is it possible that Tintin doesn't understand what the word "centered" means?" Antoine asked the room. The radiator was now installed so high up that it was no longer possible to open Antoine's newly installed window above.

"Momo wasn't lying." I ground my teeth. "Tintin really is his worst electrician. *Salaud.*"

This was a huge waste of time. We needed to get the radiators installed so I could begin painting. Six rooms - each with at least one coat of primer and two coats of paint - that was a lot of painting to do in only three weeks.

"At least there is no risk now that somebody will kick it by accident," Gégé pointed out. "You have to give him some credit for that."

Franck maintained a stony silence that we all respected. After all, Franck would have to be the one to ask Tintin to reposition the radiator for a third time.

"There's nothing further we can do right now," Antoine declared at last. "Let's have lunch."

Between my shutter painting steps I had prepared us steaks in delectable red wine sauce that was bubbling away on the stove. We devoured them while debating the best way to approach Tintin.

"Pay him compliments," I suggested.

"Tell him he works like a pig," Antoine said.

"Punch him." Gégé mopped up the last bit of sauce with his baguette.

Three sets of eyes swung to Gégé. He shrugged. "It is no more preposterous than the other ideas."

We were just cutting into a soft round cheese that Franck had bought from the monks at the nearby Cîteaux monastery when Tintin banged through the door with a second radiator – this one for the living room - in his arms. He must have grabbed it from the cellar on his way back from lunch.

"Coffee?" I asked Tintin, out of politeness, never thinking he would even acknowledge the offer.

He dumped the radiator down against the entry wall. "*Ouais*," he muttered and came in the kitchen. All of a sudden there didn't seem to be enough oxygen in the room for all of us.

I hopped up. "Take my chair. Please. I have to wash the dishes anyway."

Franck usually helped me but I didn't nag him today. My husband had bigger fish to fry and I wouldn't trade places with him for all the dirty dishes in the world. Tintin lowered his hulking form down on my chair and sipped coffee out of the delicate red espresso cup I sat down in front of him. Franck cleared his throat.

"About the radiator in the bedroom," Franck began. Gégé and Antoine exchanged an alarmed glance. Franck was going to do this now? In front of us?

"I put it up higher, like you said."

"I think maybe now it might be too high…you know…just *un petit peu.*"

Tintin narrowed his eyes.

"The problem is we can no longer open the window."

Tintin drew his black brows together. "Are you sure?"

"Definitely won't open," Antoine piped up. "We checked."

Tintin heaved his massive shoulders up, as if to say that we were downright fussy to care about trivial matters such as opening windows. He put down his espresso cup and stalked into the bedroom. Franck followed.

When he returned, Franck told us all that he actually measured and marked off for Tintin where he wanted the radiator to be placed. At the end of the day, once Tintin had departed without a word, we checked and high fived each other over the fact that Tintin actually managed to place it pretty close to Franck's markings.

"Do you think you should mark out where you want him to put the living room radiator?" Gégé asked Franck the next morning.

"I think he got the point about needing to center them," Franck said. "I don't want to compound the insult."

"Not to mention you're scared he might disembowel you," Gégé said.

"You've got that right," Franck smiled and slid his arm around my shoulders.

That day we rushed into the living room after Tintin had left for lunch. Franck had been wrong about Tintin getting the point. Although he had centered the radiator vertically he had placed it way over to the right.

"*Mon Dieu*," Franck buried his head in his hands. "I never even thought...wait! Laura, go to Claire's and buy three bottles of wine. Nice ones."

Claire's mother, in her comforting gray bun and flowered housedress, sent me home with a slightly effervescent *Aligoté*, a 1995 *Hautes-Côtes de Nuits* and a 1996 *Hautes-Côtes de Beaune – Cuvée Printemps*. The spring weather made me want to meander through the vineyards and canola fields on the way home. However, I knew I couldn't dawdle. My mission was an urgent one.

I walked in the door just in time. Tintin was shooting daggers at Franck and packing his tools in a huff. I passed Franck the carton of wine and he passed it to Tintin with a flourish.

"These are to say sorry for being such difficult clients," he said. "They're made by my friend Claire, just up the road. She's a superb winemaker."

Tintin took the bottles in his meaty hands and studied them for a time. Franck and I remained frozen. Then, for the first time since I had met him, I saw Tintin's fleshy mouth crack open into something that looked suspiciously like a smile. He nodded and set back to work with an energy akin to enthusiasm.

That evening, after installing the radiators in the living room and the blue bedroom in an admirably centered fashion, Tintin came into the kitchen while Gégé and Antoine were having their evening *kir*.

"Would you like one?" Franck asked him.

"Yes." He sat down and drummed his dusty fingers on the tabletop.

"Ah...what have you got planned for the weekend?" Gégé asked.

"I'm going to hunt wild boars."

"Really? Where?"

The conversation and Tintin became quite animated, and one drink led to three and then four.

"I make the best omelette in the world," Tin Tin boasted, the *kirs* making him downright loquacious. "Do you know what my secret is?"

Antoine leaned forward, always interested in talking about fine cooking. "Truffles?"

"*Non*! Boar's blood. Just a few spoonfuls."

"Really?" asked Franck. "I wouldn't have guessed."

"If I make a kill this weekend I'll have you all over to taste one of my omelettes," Tin Tin promised.

Franck's eyes opened wide. "Wow. *Merci.*" I was touched, but sent a silent prayer to the Virgin Mary statue across the street that TinTin would return from his next hunting trip empty-handed.

After he left we all sat in stupefaction.

"Three glasses of *kir* and it was like he had a personality transplant," I mused. "Incredible."

"Five," Franck corrected me. "And I was rather heavy-handed with the *cassis* liqueur."

"Not that incredible." Antoine shrugged. "All anyone needs is to feel appreciated for what they do."

CHAPTER 24

A few days later I woke up and, unusual for me, bounced out of our sofa bed. Antoine had finished installing our new windows and he was going to start building our bookshelf in the fireplace. Better yet, I had finished the boring white undercoat in the far bedroom at around midnight the previous night and now I could actually begin painting the walls with color.

The color I picked for the bedroom – a lovely crisp Granny Apple green – was not a color that one sees on walls in France (or anywhere else, for that matter) very often. When Franck brought the paint pot home from the store I pried open the lid immediately. My breath caught at its beauty. Franck and Gégé had just stared down at the paint.

Gégé nudged Franck. "Glad you'll be sleeping in the room, not me."

"I don't think I'll be able to actually sleep in a room that color," Franck said. "It tickles my brain."

Pushing their doubt out of my mind I walked across the cool tile and flung open the shutters. The dawn was pink and promising and the *tilleuls* in front of the church had burst into life with a profusion of baby leaves. It was a perfect day for my colour green.

I almost danced back to the bed to wake up Franck, but I was greeted with a moan.

"What's wrong?"

"I'm dying."

I went in the bathroom in search of our thermometer. Franck had looked pale yesterday and had been dragging his sander around as though it weighed a hundred pounds. I found the thermometer and brought it back to our sofa bed where Franck was curled in a fetal position.

"How does dying feel exactly?"

"I ache all over. My throat is on fire and my head feels like it's being squeezed in a vice."

"Open your mouth so I can take your temperature."

"No," he said. "I know I have a fever."

I sighed. Franck didn't get sick very often - almost never actually - but when he did he was difficult in the way of people who enjoy almost perfect health. He was always incredulous and resentful of the fact that a virus would dare bring him down.

"Come on," I coaxed. "Open your mouth and let me stick this in, then I'll make your breakfast for you."

"I'm not hungry. Or thirsty." While he was talking I managed to slip the thermometer under his tongue.

When it beeped, it read 39 degrees Celsius. Definitely a temperature. I went in the bathroom and rummaged through the shelves but realized we didn't have any aspirin.

"I'm calling Docteur DuPont," I announced as I returned to the living room.

"*Non,*" Franck groaned but I had already begun to dial. They had an appointment available in thirty minutes' time. *Parfait.* I bustled Franck into some clothes and out of the door just as Gégé and Antoine let themselves in the veranda.

"Franck's sick," I announced. "He's going to the doctor right now."

"She's making me." Franck rolled his eyes in my direction.

They clucked in commiseration and Franck cast me a dark look. "I'm sure it was the idea of that green color in the bedroom that made me sick," he muttered.

Gégé, Antoine and I decided to have our breakfast on the sunny stone steps while we waited for Franck. We were licking up the last crumbs from our *pains au chocolat* when Franck's footsteps crunched on the gravel under the passageway.

My husband settled down on a step below me, carrying a huge plastic bag emblazoned with the unmistakable green pharmacy insignia. The size of the bag didn't take me by surprise. The first time I got sick in France – a run-of-the-mill cold when I was only eighteen and a Rotary exchange student - my host mother in Nuits-Saint-Georges called her doctor who made a house call and prescribed a dizzying array of seven different medications for me. In Canada I would have been told to go home, drink a lot of orange juice, and maybe take a vitamin C tablet. One box contained pills so huge that I couldn't figure out how I was possibly going to swallow them until my host brother explained to me with the help of some very urgent hand miming that they were actually suppositories. I didn't take any of the medicine, especially not the suppositories, but I got better anyway.

"What did the doctor say?" I asked, kneading the rigid muscles of Franck's shoulders.

"He says I've caught a cold in my stomach," Franck said, leaning his head back in my lap and picking up the last *croissant*.

"A what?"

"A cold in my stomach. You always steal the covers at night, so *voilà*! Now I have caught a cold in my stomach." Franck's theory was preposterous, but at least he wasn't still blaming it on my choice of green paint.

"You can't catch a cold in your *stomach*."

Franck coughed to prove that yes, you could.

"Gégé?" I arched an eyebrow at him for some back-up.

"I catch cold in my stomach every winter," Gégé said.

"So do I," Antoine said. "It is the worst place to catch cold. What did he give you?" Their faces perked up like they did when they delved into a profound debate about plumbing valves. They started to rifle enthusiastically through Franck's pharmaceutical loot bag.

"These ones mop up anything," I heard Gégé say, reading the label of Franck's box of antibiotics. "They give me terrible diarrhoea though."

I shook my head at the lot of them and went to the bedroom.

My breath caught as I poured a ribbon of crisp, chlorophyll-filled color into the paint pan and dipped in my brush. Corners and edges first, then I could go whole hog with the roller.

Ten minutes later any doubts I harbored had vanished. The green completely transformed the room. I couldn't remember the last time I had done something so satisfying. My brushing fell into a meditative rhythm and my thoughts began to wander. I could still hear Franck coughing and sniffing in the kitchen. I didn't believe in the existence of stomach colds but I hated to see him so sick. My husband had such an incredible capacity for hard and sustained physical labour that sometimes I forgot that his body also had limits to what it could endure. Of course he had hit the wall. If it had been anyone else besides Franck doing all the plastering and lifting and troubleshooting they would have hit the wall two months ago. In our couple I was the one with the crazy ideas and the ability to sell them to those around me but Franck was the one who threw body and mind into making them happen. We were a pretty effective team, although today it hit home how much I needed him by my side to move forward on our project. We were racing down the final stretch and couldn't afford any casualties, but *especially* not Franck. There was no way we could finish without him.

I attacked another corner. It was scary to depend so much on someone else. I ruminated on this for a few minutes and then it dawned on me that at Oxford I had been independent. During those two years I had relied on no one but myself…and I had been miserable with the isolation.

Franck and I were a team again. Franck couldn't finish this house without me any more than I could finish it without him. We both needed Gégé and Antoine, and even Paulo and the enigmatic Tintin. We were all locked together in this project. It was still possible that we were locked into a huge disaster, but the bottom line was we all needed each other.

I was hard at work on my final wall when I heard the chatter of voices from the street below.

"What do you think it means?" I heard one person say.

"I have never seen anything - " another began.

"Can you just imagine what Marthe would say?" a third voice interrupted.

I went and leaned out the window. Gathered out in the middle of the road in front of our house was a band of villagers, not people who I saw together very often but who must have been out strolling around enjoying the warm spring air.

"*Bonjour!*" I called out, my bright green paintbrush over my shoulder. "What do you think of the new colour?"

They fell silent.

"I'd better get back to work," I said. "Just wait until you see the colour of the shutters!"

With a wide grin I left them to their gossip and continued painting. I started rolling paint on the walls with the big roller. My arm soon felt like it was going to fall off, but I kept painting. Gégé came in to take a break from plumbing the kitchen sink and check on my progress.

"What do you think?" I surveyed my work. Almost three quarters of the walls were now green. "Is it growing on you?"

"*Non.* Definitely not.*"

"Not even *un petit peu*?"

"I do believe that you may be *un petit peu* insane," he conceded.

Franck coughed his way into the room, one hand crossed over his stomach to protect the cold in there. His eyes widened as he took in the walls and he clutched his head. "Arghhhhhh," he moaned. "Why do I let you make such crazy decisions?"

"You'll love it," I said. "Eventually." I put my roller down and went over to give him a kiss.

"Careful," he said afterwards. "I don't want to get you sick."

"You won't. This green colour seems to have medicinal properties for me." I pivoted him around. "Now go and try to rest in the living room."

"Antoine is building our bookshelf in there. I'll just have to drag around today and do what I can. Aren't you worried about getting finished in time?"

I shrugged. "I figure that one way or another we will finish. We have no choice."

"I just don't see how we're going to get from where we are today to finished." Franck massaged his forehead.

"We don't need to see how in order to do it," I said.

"Hmmmm." Franck walked out of the room. "I think my wife is becoming a philosopher."

Mid-afternoon somebody knocked timidly on the bedroom door

where I was working on my second coat. I turned around to see André, Franck's father, glancing around the room with a stunned look on his face.

"*Bonjour!*" I said and went over to give him *les bises.*

"You've been working hard," he observed.

"*Oui.* What do you think of the color?"

He blinked several times and cleared his throat. He finally patted my shoulder.

"Don't worry, Laura. I'm certain it won't look quite so green when there's furniture in the room." André gave the room one last horrified look and then departed.

I studied the color again. I didn't seem to be seeing it with the same eyes as the others. I loved it. Could I continue loving it knowing how much everyone hated it?

Franck came back in. "*Mon dieu.* I didn't think the color could be as bad as I remembered but it's actually worse."

"It's just paint."

"I'm sure I will never be able to sleep in here."

"It will be dark. Your eyes will be closed."

"What about when we're in bed during the day? I'm not sure I can do you justice surrounded by this color."

"I'm not worried about that."

He crossed his arms and sighed but the corner of his mouth twitched. "I suppose we'll just have to work at it."

"I'm game," I said. "But not right this second. I have to finish this coat before it dries."

I needed to trust my instincts. Maybe nobody could see the beauty of my color choice yet but, just like the house when we had purchased it, that didn't mean beauty wasn't there.

Antoine was the only one who didn't have just bad things to say about my paint color. It was "*très original*" according to him.

Half way into my second coat I felt like my back was going to snap in two if I didn't stretch it out. I meandered into the living room where he was cutting shelves for the bookcase in the fireplace. I admired the precision of his movements.

"How is the painting going?" he asked.

"Good," I said. "Except that everyone but me and you hates the color." He shrugged, as if to say this was small potatoes indeed.

"Is the other bedroom next?"

"I think I'll paint the kitchen buffet after, while it's nice out. Who knows how long this hot weather is going to last."

He plucked his pencil from behind his ear and made a mark on the piece of wood he was working on. "What color will you paint it?"

"White. I love the lines of the buffet, but that *faux* wood varnish that Marthe must have painted it with is horrific."

Antoine laughed. "That varnish was all the rage thirty years ago. You're going to have a rough time trying to paint over it. It repels every substance known to man."

I decided this wasn't really worth contemplating at the moment and gazed around the room while I did a few backstretches. My eyes wandered over to the living room buffet.

"*That* monster" - I nodded over to it - "is going straight to the antique dealer as soon as we can find enough people to help us squeeze it through the door."

Antoine stopped his measuring. "*Quoi?* How can you say that? That buffet is by far the most beautiful piece of furniture here."

"Seriously? You really think that? It gives me nightmares."

Antoine held out his hand to me. "Come here," he said, and led me over to the buffet. He put my hand down on the wood top and motioned at me to stroke it. The wood felt silky and smooth under my fingertips.

"It is carved out of pear wood I believe," he said. He pulled out a drawer and pointed to the tight fitting tongue and groove joints. "Have you noticed this? There's not a nail in this whole thing and yet it fits together like a perfectly crafted puzzle. Can you imagine the skill of the person who carved it? It's old too."

"It is?"

Antoine ran his fingers down the glass fronts of the two upper cabinets. "Look closely," he ordered. "Do you see the tiny bubbles? This isn't manufactured glass, it was pulled by hand."

There were tiny bubbles in there, caught in the wavy glass. They were quite fascinating actually. "I never noticed those before."

"If I were to hazard a guess I would say this dates back to the mid 1800's. It is without a doubt the most exquisite and oldest piece you have in this house. Do me a favour – don't sell it yet. Think about it for a bit longer."

"*D'accord*," I found myself agreeing and ran my hand over the wood again. "I'll wait a bit longer." Maybe I too could be blind to beauty right in front of me.

CHAPTER 25

The sun rose hot on our last day. I sipped my morning *café au lait* on the stone stairs and turned my face up like a sunflower to the warmth of the spring sunshine. The lavender planted in the dirt below seemed to have doubled in size during the night as I had slept. A riot of sweet peas had sprung up from nowhere.

Tomorrow we'd be leaving for Oxford to attend my graduation ceremony with my parents. I would find myself on that same TGV I had arrived on back in June, winding its way North through the French countryside. My graduation was on May 1st and Franck and I had already planned to wake up early that day and go to listen to the choir singing at the top of Magdalen tower at six o'clock in the morning, something I had always wanted to do but had never managed in our two years living there.

I was surprised to find myself looking forward to returning to Oxford. I thought I would be haunted forever by the confusion and despair that had circled within me as I climbed those stairs of the Examination Schools to write my final exams. Yet sometime over the past several months - even though I couldn't for the life of me pinpoint exactly when - a sense of pride had taken their place. I was proud of the fact that I had survived my two years at Oxford, but I was prouder still of the little voice inside me that had told me to say "*non!*" to Mr. Partridge. That voice had gotten louder over the past little while, perhaps a bit cocky even. After all, the house was finished. We had done it.

The freshly painted metal door of the veranda opened behind me. I turned around to see Franck dressed in a paint splattered T-shirt and a ratty pair of cut-offs. We had hardly brought any nice clothes when we had come here to do the renovations and both of our wardrobes had been reduced to dirty tatters.

"Do you think we have enough *Merguez*?" he asked, sounding worried. We had bought about sixty *merguez* sausages as well as sixty *chipolatas* which amounted to about five a person but still, Franck had inherited his Mémé's terror of inviting people over to dinner and not having enough to eat.

"Definitely," I said, patting the stone step beside me. "Come sit with me."

"When I get back. I have to go and get the cases of wine for Gégé and Antoine." He bounced down the steps in the morning sun, the cold in his stomach a distant memory. "Then I have to pick up the baguettes."

We had ordered twenty baguettes for our celebratory barbeque at noon that day. It was absolutely essential, according to Gégé and Franck, that we baptize the house with a copious amount of eating and drinking. To miss this crucial step, apparently, would be cursing our home for years to come.

I reluctantly picked up my empty bowl and stood up. "I guess I'd better get back to work." I blew Franck a kiss that he lifted up his hand and caught with quick fingers. "*A toute à l'heure.*"

I wandered into the living room and sat down in front of the computer that I had set up on the dining room table. Some last minute touches still had to be completed; I had about twenty more pages to add before the information binder I was leaving for our guests was complete. I had to pack up my computer and the clothes and the remnant detritus we weren't taking with us and put them in a box in the basement...

My fingers lifted up from the keyboard and I drank in the room around me. There was no denying it – the dream of our French house that had flitted in and out of my mind's eye this past year had become a reality. The crooked walls were freshly plastered and painted with fresh ivory paint, my cheese cabinet had been pampered and cleaned and oiled into its former glory, the ancient concrete tiles at my feet were maybe not stain free – given that they were over one hundred years old

I doubted they would ever be that again – but they were gleaming from yesterday's cleaning.

All this had been accomplished even though most of the time I hadn't been able to see anything past my next breath, let alone any grand vision. Yet this potential had been in this house all along and the potential for unlocking it had been in *us* all along, even during those days when we felt lost and like we had made a huge mistake. We hadn't known where we were going but we still ended up somewhere wonderful in the end.

I shook my head at the miracle that surrounded me and got back to work.

Later on the sun had risen even higher and hotter when I carried the last box of our personal items down to the cellar. In the cellar's cool air I moved a pair of peeling shutters that leaned against the wall to make space to put down my box. Behind them was not a wall as I had expected, but a door. It was very old with battered wood and *"Café"* painted in large black letters. I opened it up to reveal a wall of stone between the street and me. How odd. This house hadn't finished sharing its quirks and mysteries with us.

I grabbed two garden chairs for our soon-to-be-arriving guests and manoeuvred through the cellar door that led out to the passageway, silently thanking the forward thinking stonemason who had carved the stone a little wider to be able to roll the wine barrels in and out of the cellar. Turned out it was handy for garden chairs as well.

"La Lolo!" Gégé called out as he crunched his way across the pea gravel towards me. I put my chairs down and we gave each other affectionate *bises*. I caught a whiff of *Savon de Marseille* in his freshly pressed shirt collar and tears welled up in my eyes. I would miss having Gégé arrive on our doorstep almost every morning with his wry smile and his insatiable appetite for lost causes (not to mention the *pains au chocolat*).

"Let me help you." He took the chairs I was carrying. I wrestled one back from him and he rolled his eyes at me.

"You know Gégé," I said, "we couldn't have done this without - "

"Is that showerhead working better now?" he interrupted, blushing garnet. "Maybe I should go and have a look at - "

"It's working perfectly," I said. "I checked it this morning. Today you're supposed to just relax and let us serve you food and wine."

Gégé looked distinctly unseduced by this prospect. I laughed.

"Can you believe we actually did it?"

"*Non*," Gégé said, with more than a tinge of regret in his voice. I truly think that although he was happy for us, he was already nostalgic for our permanent state of crisis.

"It seemed impossible, didn't it?"

"Completely." We picked up our chairs and walked out from under the passageway into the sunshine. Gégé stopped by the foot of the stairs and took a moment to take in the thriving heads of lavender and the freshly painted shutters flung open to allow a peek of the bright white paint on the walls of the veranda.

Gégé let out an epic sigh. "I guess there really isn't anything else for me to do."

"Until we buy our next ruin over here," I joked.

"Are you going to do that?" he asked, his eyes shining.

I blinked. The words had just popped out, kind of like my "*non*" to Mr. Partridge, my Oxford tutor. I hadn't ever contemplated having more than one house over here before.

"Who knows?" I shrugged, and in an instant a hundred new possibilities unfolded in front of me.

The barbeque was turning out to be a huge success. All the key elements to a good French party were there: multiple generations, copious amounts of food, and delicious local wine.

Tom crawled around underfoot in brightly striped red and blue overalls, making a determined effort to put as many pieces of pea gravel in his mouth as possible. Mémé was there too. She couldn't stop exclaiming over the transformation of our house and revelled in the brilliance of Franck, one of her favourite grandsons. There were more than enough *merguez* and *chipolatas* for everyone, even though they were being devoured as soon as Franck took them off the barbeque. I served them up on old metal serving platters of Marthe's that I had unearthed (and thoroughly washed, not forgetting those quips about her love of rat poison) from the attic.

Bottle after bottle of Claire's sublime *Hautes Côte de Nuits* and *Hautes Côte de Beaune* were opened. My father – who had arrived with my mother a week before to help us down the final stretch - in particular seemed to be enjoying the beverage selection. He radiated relief that we had actually pulled through and celebrated with glass after delicious glass… maybe not such a good idea under the beating afternoon sun.

We all took turns taking Tom and Marcel, Olivier's son, for circular rides around the courtyard in an old blue wooden cart that Franck had found tucked in a little empty space under the stone stairs. Then we would collapse back down again and nibble on the platter of *Époisses* and *Cîteaux* and *Comté* that I had set out on Marthe's wooden cutting board polished with years of use.

Just as I was ready to take the cheese course back into the kitchen, my dad offered to do it and didn't come out of the house again. When I eventually went back inside to fetch the pear and apple tarts that Mémé had made for us, I found him in a snoring lump on one of the twin beds in the now blue bedroom. I couldn't believe that neither Franck nor I had collapsed yet – we had been working day and night to reach the finish line of our French House. Still, our house seemed to give back every ounce of our energy and love that we poured into it, buoying both of us above mundane considerations of fatigue.

As we were sipping our after-lunch espresso, various members of Franck's family began to drop by and Mémé would whisk them off to give them a tour of *La Maison des Deux Clochers*. She would twinkle up the stone stairs with her latest batch of visitors in tow, and then proceed to lead them from room to room, pointing out Franck's expert plastering job and the regal buffet in the living room that we had decided to keep after all, and which she had spent hours polishing until it appeared to gleam with a light of its own. On the way back outside she would point out my father – snoring on the bed in the blue bedroom because "he had worked so hard and perhaps had drunk a bit too much wine".

At the end of the day we all gathered back in the garden, made a toast with flutes of Claire's *crémant*, and planted the beautiful clematis that Antoine had brought us as a housewarming gift in the old stone border at the back of the garden.

We had done it.

It had seemed impossible, but somehow we had stumbled along and showed up every day, even on the days (and there were many) when we were feeling tired and disheartened. Just the act of continuing at the times when I felt utterly paralysed by doubt…wasn't that a kind of faith in and of itself? It was definitely not as picturesque as Franck's panoply of guardian angels, but I held on to it like a turquoise cat's eye marble that I had once discovered mysteriously in my pocket when I was eight. I didn't know how it got there. I didn't know where it came from. I did know, however, that it was precious and that it was mine.

That evening, once my parents had gone to bed, Franck and I snuck outside for one last moment to savor the warmth of the evening. The stone steps cooled the back of my thighs. Franck settled beside me and his arm stole around my shoulder. A wave of joy swept over me, so powerful that I had to wrap my fingers around the freshly painted lavender banister to steady myself.

"It's funny," I said to Franck in a low voice so as not to waken my exhausted parents. "Since I can remember, I've always felt as though I needed to know where I was headed. I don't feel that way anymore."

"What's changed?"

"This house. Us." I nestled my head in the crook of his neck. "All these months, I didn't know where I was going. Most of the time I felt completely lost, but it turned out that didn't matter in the end. We still ended up here. We still ended up in this moment, right now."

Franck twirled my ponytail around his finger. "How would you describe this moment?"

I soaked in the orange evening sky and the smell of the fresh leaves on the grapevine growing beside me on the railing and the solid stone of our house underneath me.

"Perfect."

Even though life was never perfect, certain moments were.

The clock on the church tower began to ring out the *Angelus*. I kissed Franck. The powerful notes made the metal vibrate under my fingertips. If life hadn't been so complicated and messy I would never have stumbled my way here.

"I think I'm ready to have a baby," I blurted out.

Franck laughed. "Since when?"

I kissed him again, more soundly this time. "Since right this instant."

FIN

MERCI

My Grape Escape is the result of the help and support from so many wonderful people. First of all, *un énorme merci* to my wonderful husband who puts up with me writing about him. He has never sought the spotlight but loves me enough to allow me to shine it on him regardless. He swept me off my feet twenty-two years ago and continues to do so every day.

Thanks to my girls for never doubting for a second that I would publish my book in the end and for always asking me how it was coming along, even on days when it felt like a distant pipe dream. Charlotte, Camille, and Clémentine are, without a doubt, my finest and most miraculous creations.

An enormous *bisous* to Pam and Lisa, the best editors and cheerleaders a writer could ever wish for and to Daisy for all her savvy design expertise. *Merci* to all my beloved girlfriends and family members for always having my back.

Thank you so much to *mon amie* Marjorie Taylor of The Cook's Atelier in Beaune for allowing me to use a photo of her vintage Citroën (named 'Madeleine') for my cover. If you ever want a sublime cooking course or market tour in Beaune, look up Marjorie at www.thecooksatelier.com or visit her Epicurean center at 42, rue de Lorraine.

I truly owe a debt to Nicolas for telling me I just needed to finish one – any one - of my *putains de livres* so I could learn how to let go. Also, to Sukumar who got me unstuck by suggesting that I start at the end, and to all the writers who participate in the Surrey International Writer's Conference for being such an inspiring, crazy, and supportive tribe.

"Cheers" to my Oxford tutor who told me that my writing was lovely, even though my legal reasoning was utter rubbish.

A huge thanks to all my friends at the PSC Partners Facebook forum. You have made the path of being diagnosed with a rare and unpredictable disease so much more bearable. To Philip Burke and Sandi Pearlman – I feel so fortunate that I was able to benefit from your caring, warmth, and knowledge before you passed over. Rest in

Peace *mes amis* – you made a difference in some of the darkest days of my life that will never be forgotten. Ten per cent of the royalties from this and any of my future books will be donated back to PSC Partners Seeking A Cure and earmarked for research. Everybody, please sign up to be an organ donor and campaign to have "opt-out" organ donation policies adopted throughout the world. Too many precious lives like Philip's and Sandi's are being lost every day due to inertia.

Lastly, *merci, merci, merci* to all our guests who have stayed at **La Maison des Deux Clochers** over the past fourteen years. Your enthusiasm for Burgundy, your love for the authentic, and your appreciation for the simple pleasures of life in France are the reason why Franck and I love what we do and the inspiration for us to continue to grow our vacation rental network in Burgundy (www.graperentals.com). You inspired me to write this book and you are and always will be an integral part of our story.

Read on for a sneak peek at *My Grape Village*, the sequel to the bestselling *My Grape Escape*.

CHAPTER 1

"Are they going to survive?" I asked Franck.

I clutched the metal gate as I watched our two daughters make their way through the preschool playground. I had never seen such a place of utter lawlessness.

Despite the larger than life statue of the Virgin Mary that loomed over the courtyard, French children punched and taunted each other. Here was the *laissez-faire* philosophy in action. A cluster of teachers stood well off to the side of the mayhem. They chatted and sipped, espressos out of china cups. It would have been entertaining to watch if not for the fact that Franck and I had just jettisoned our daughters into the deep end of it all.

Two and a half year old Camille in her yellow sundress and white sandals glanced back at us and furrowed her eyebrows. She lowered her head and marched straight to her classroom door, making eye contact with no-one. She disappeared inside. I couldn't take it, I had to make sure-

I opened the gate, and winced as the rusty metal screeched.

"*Non Madame Germain!*" One of the teachers in the cluster shook her finger at me. "No parents allowed in the courtyard during school hours!"

"How did she see me?" I turned to Franck. "She didn't even turn around when that red -haired kid beat that other little boy to a pulp."

"They see what they want to see," Franck said, putting his hand over mine as he closed the gate. There was more metallic squealing and the teachers heads all snapped in our direction.

"I bet they don't oil the gate on purpose," I muttered. I glanced down at Franck's hand over mine. His knuckles were white.

"*Allez,*" he said. "We must leave them."

I caught sight of four and a half year old Charlotte walking to her classroom, located at the far end of the schoolyard. Her blond hair was pulled up with two ladybug barrettes and she rolled a *cartable* – her

French school bag - behind her. She smiled at a little boy wearing a chic little mint green Lacoste polo shirt who ran toward her. He shoved her as he ran past, knocking over both her and her *cartable*. Charlotte picked herself up. She looked stricken for a moment and then continued to walk to her class again with a brave smile plastered on her face. A girl with angelic blond braids had the temerity to stick her tongue out at my precious eldest daughter. Charlotte blinked back tears and when she reached the classroom door gave us a small wave that was so courageous it splintered my heart in two.

Franck dragged me back up the path and out the heavy wooden doors of the school. The doors were promptly locked behind us.

Once we were in the parking lot I threw myself against his chest. "We've made a terrible mistake," I mumbled into his T-shirt.

The girls weren't even supposed to be going to Saint Coeur, or Sainted Heart, in Beaune. They had been signed up to attend the village schools in Magny-les-Villers and Villers-la-Faye. Three days ago, a teacher friend of Franck's phoned to tell him they couldn't take Charlotte. There were simply too many children in her year. We scrambled to find a school for the girls so we could have time to work. Franck thought of Saint Coeur because it was where I went to school during my year as a Rotary exchange student in Burgundy when I was seventeen. They luckily – or so I thought at the time – had spots for both of our daughters. Now I knew the truth. Saint Coeur wasn't full like other schools because this place was where Burgundian society put all the hardened future criminals.

Franck kissed the top of my head. "We just need to give it time Laura. We all have to adapt. I went to preschool in France and, *régardez!* I'm still here."

I stared at the locked doors. "I can't stand the thought of my girls trapped in there with all of those horrible French children and the teachers who don't care if they get kill…"

"We had good reasons for moving back to France," Franck interrupted. "Not just for us, but for them."

Maybe we did, but my daydreams of familial bonding at Beaune's Saturday market, introducing the girls to *pain au chocolat* and *escargots*, and becoming fluent in French had shriveled up in the last ten minutes.

"I can't remember why those reasons were so compelling, can you?" I asked Franck.

"Not at the moment, to be honest." Franck glanced at the closed doors and frowned. "I do know one thing though."

"What?"

"Stéphanie told me about a Judo class that Tom takes. I'm going to sign our girls up right away."

"I never thought self-defense was something the girls would have to learn over here."

Franck pulled me towards the car. "It may be the most important thing," he said.

Made in the USA
Charleston, SC
21 October 2014